THE KISS OF CHRIST

NICK PADOVANI

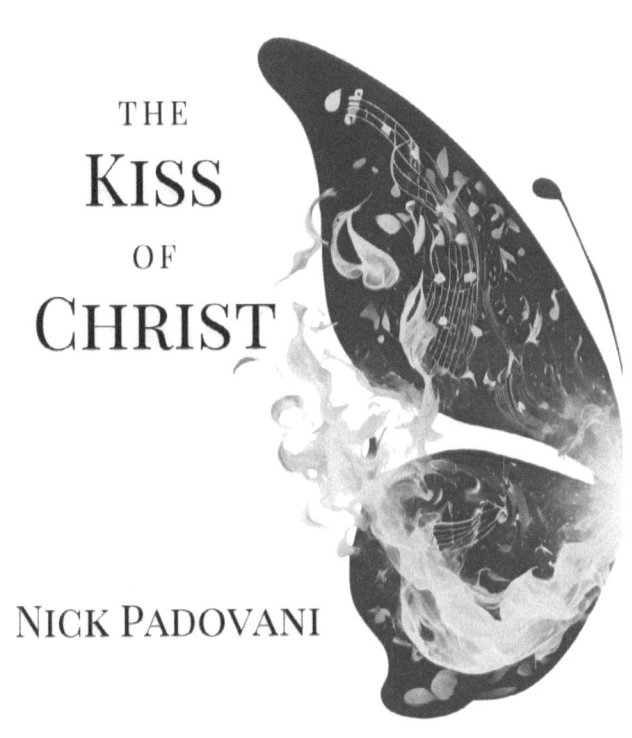

Copyright © 2025 by Nick Padovani

THE KISS OF CHRIST
Nick Padovani

Published by **Eyes Open Press**
www.eyesopenpress.com

Printed in the United States of America
ISBN-13: 978-1-7360733-7-7 (paperback)
ISBN-13: 978-1-7360733-8-4 (e-book)
Library of Congress Control Number: 2025915758

All rights reserved. No part of this publication may be reproduced, stored in a retrieval system, or transmitted in any form or by any means—electronic, mechanical, photocopy, recording, or otherwise—without the prior written permission of the author, except in the case of brief quotations used in articles, reviews, or scholarly works.

Scripture quotations, unless otherwise indicated, are taken from the
New American Standard Bible® (1995 edition).
Copyright © 1960, 1971, 1977, 1995 by The Lockman Foundation.
Used by permission. All rights reserved. Lockman.org

Scripture quotations marked **TPT** are from *The Passion Translation®.*
Copyright © 2017, 2018, 2020 by Passion & Fire Ministries, Inc.
Used by permission. All rights reserved. ThePassionTranslation.com

Scripture quotations marked **NIV** are taken from the *Holy Bible, New International Version®.* Copyright © 1973, 1978, 1984, 2011 by Biblica, Inc.™
Used by permission. All rights reserved worldwide.

Scripture quotations marked **NKJV** are taken from the *New King James Version®.* Copyright © 1982 by Thomas Nelson.
Used by permission. All rights reserved.

Scripture quotations marked **PHILLIPS** are from the *New Testament in Modern English* by J.B. Phillips. Copyright © J.B. Phillips 1958, 1960, 1972.
Used by permission of Macmillan Publishing Co., Inc. All rights reserved.

Scripture quotations marked **HPB** are from the *Hawaiian Pidgin Bible*
©2020 Hawaii Pidgin Bible Ministries. Hawaiipidginbible.org

To my friends and family at *The Almond Branch* who have walked with me in the rhythms of grace.

Thank you for saying yes to the dance of the Divine Family.

CONTENTS

Acknowledgements   vii
Foreword   ix
Prelude: *Getting Oriented*   xiii

MOVEMENT ONE: TREASURE
Day 1: Revelation   3
Day 2: Strings   7
Day 3: Trinity   11
Day 4: Quartet   17
Day 5: Blessing   21
Day 6: Lightning   27
Day 7: Kiss   33
   Selah   39

MOVEMENT TWO: DISCORD
Day 8: Broken Identity   43
Day 9: Religion's Song   49
Day 10: The Harlot   53
Day 11: The Table   59
Day 12: Hidden Glory   65
Day 13: Sensory Experience   71
Day 14: New Wine   77
   Selah   83

MOVEMENT THREE: AWAKE
Day 15: A Lingering Spell   87
Day 16: A Fractured Wall   93
Day 17: The Awake Tree   99
Day 18: Fox and Dove   105
Day 19: Babylon and Zion   111
Day 20: Fire and Gladness   117
Day 21: It is Finished   123
   Selah   129

MOVEMENT FOUR: HARMONY

    Day 22: The Vulnerability of God — 133
    Day 23: Communion and the Door — 139
    Day 24: The Mystery and Tension — 143
    Day 25: Crescendo of the Song — 149
    Day 26: When the Light Dawns — 155
    Day 27: Our Calling and Destiny — 161
    Day 28: Rising from the Wilderness — 167
      Selah — 175

Overture: *Scavenger Hunt (Back) to Jerusalem* — 177
Go Deeper into the Song — 179
Author Bio — 181

Acknowledgements

First, I want to thank my wife, Kelly. You are my best friend—a wellspring of joy and healing in my life.

I also want to thank Dr. Brian Simmons for your pioneering work on the Song of Songs. Your labor of love in biblical translation was built upon many years of faithful service in the Kingdom, opening the way for countless others to encounter the deeper affections of God's heart. Thank you for your encouragement in my own journey as a writer.

And to Dylan—my brother and friend—thank you for standing by my side as a constant voice of inspiration.

And finally, the most important acknowledgement …

… to the acknowledgement of the mystery of God, and of the Father, and of Christ; in whom are hid all the treasures of wisdom and knowledge.
–Colossians 2:2-3 KJV–

The Mystery has captivated my heart and nudged me every step of the way as I've written this book. May the reader come to discover its glory as well—and the riches it brings.

More on that in a moment…

FOREWORD

In every corner of creation, we can sense the divine melody that stirs the deepest recesses of the human heart. It is a sound both ancient and new, familiar and mysterious, calling us back to something we have longed for and forgotten in equal measure. It is the Song of the Ages—the Song of God's heart, sung over each one of us since the beginning of time. This Song has a voice, and within that voice, there is a kiss. A kiss with the power to awaken, heal, and transform.

In *The Kiss of Christ*, Nick Padovani has captured the profound beauty of this Song in a way that allows us, the readers, to hear its divine cadence and enter its sacred dance. Through the pages of this book, we are invited to move beyond the shadows and into the brilliance of God's eternal light. As we journey with Padovani through the poetry of Solomon's *Song of Songs*, we are not merely learning about love—we are experiencing it. Not just love as we know it, but divine love—a love that calls us to abandon our fears, our walls of insecurity, and the chains of religious duty that so often keep us from the full expression of God's heart.

God loves to sing. It is an expression of His joy, His delight, His passion for His creation. But He also loves to sing over us—each of us, individually. He sings in the quiet of the morning, in the depths of our darkest moments, and in the rhythm of our daily lives. And if we will stop long enough to listen—if we quiet our hearts enough to hear—we will catch the melodies of His grace. These are not mere words—they are the very breath of life, a breath that gives us strength to overcome, wisdom to see, and love to live. The Song of the Ages is an anthem, an eternal love song that transcends all time and space, and in it, we find the very essence of our being.

In these pages, Nick Padovani opens up the mysteries of Solomon's Song in a way that will captivate your heart and spirit. He brings the lyrics of this ancient ballad to life, revealing layers of meaning often missed or misunderstood. This is not simply a romantic poem of love—it is a divine love story, the story of God's relentless pursuit of His bride. As you read, you will find yourself drawn into the beauty of this love story, where every word is a tender whisper from the heart of God, calling you deeper into His embrace.

There is something deeply freeing about the message Padovani conveys. Throughout the history of faith, people have often been burdened by the weight of religion—the rules, the rituals, the expectations. It is easy to forget that God did not come to burden us but to set us free. Religion, in its purest form, was never meant to be a weight to bear but a pathway to intimacy with God. The Song that Padovani speaks of is not one of burden but of freedom—a Song that lifts our spirits, heals the wounds of our past, and transforms our hearts.

When we talk about the "kiss of Christ," we speak of something far more profound than a simple gesture. This kiss is the expression of a love that knows no bounds. It is the kiss of grace—the kiss that brings us into our union with Christ, the kiss that transforms us from the inside out. It is a kiss that calls us to leave behind the darkness of hiding, the walls of shame and fear, and to step boldly into the light of His love. The kiss of Christ is the invitation to become one with Him—to enter into the sacred dance of love that He has long been waiting for us to join.

Padovani's exploration of the Song of Songs is more than an intellectual exercise—it is a spiritual experience. As you read, you will begin to sense the tender touch of God's Spirit drawing you closer to Himself. You will hear the melody of the Song, and within that melody, you will find healing, renewal, and joy. This is not simply a call to understand God's love, but an invitation to experience it in a way that will change you forever.

The journey Nick Padovani invites us on is not one that can be completed by intellectual assent alone. It is a journey of the heart—one that requires us to open ourselves up to the presence of God in a fresh and powerful way. When we enter into the Song of the Ages, we step into a world of beauty, mystery, and longing—a world that invites us to know God intimately and to respond to His love with every fiber of our being. This is a love that knows no end, a love that calls us to live in a way that is utterly surrendered to Him.

As you read *The Kiss of Christ*, you will find that you are not only learning about God's love—you are encountering it. You will discover the richness of His presence, the depth of His affection, and the power of His grace. And as you do, you will find yourself drawn into the eternal dance of the Song of the Ages, where every step is filled with the grace, beauty, and freedom of Christ's love.

In these last days, as darkness seems to sweep across the nations, the Song of the Ages becomes more vital than ever. It is the Song that will pierce through the darkness, offering light and hope to all who are willing to listen. We live in a time when the world is desperate for love—a love that is pure, enduring, and all-consuming. This Song, sung by our Bridegroom, is the answer to the longing of every heart. It is the Song that will transform lives, renew minds, and restore souls.

As you read this book, let your heart be open to the melody Nick Padovani so beautifully unfolds. Let the Song of the Ages become the Song of your life, and let the kiss of Christ be the touch that awakens your soul to the fullness of His love. You will never be the same again. This is not just a book to read—it is a journey to take, a transformation to undergo, and a love to embrace.

So, as you begin this journey through *The Kiss of Christ*, know that you are being invited into something much greater than just an exploration of scripture. You are being invited into an experience of God's heart—a heart that is bursting with love for you. As you listen to the Song of the Ages, you will find yourself dancing to its rhythm, caught up in the embrace of a love that will never let you go.

Get ready for a change—a transformation that will awaken your heart to the passion and beauty of God's love. The Song of the Ages is waiting for you. Will you hear it? Will you dance to its melody? Will you allow the kiss of Christ to awaken your soul to the fullness of His love?

I am confident that, as you read *The Kiss of Christ*, your answer will be a resounding "yes."

Dr. Brian Simmons
The Passion Translation Project

Prelude: Getting Oriented

Any true artist—whether they know God or not—has an inner antenna that can tap into the spiritual realm and pick up on certain messages that become infused into their art. The pen is particularly good at capturing spiritual truths by transcribing them symbolically into stories. This happens all the time in television scripts, movies, and literature.

J.R.R. Tolkien, someone who did indeed know God, is an example of a writer who tapped into something bigger than he perhaps intended. In *The Silmarillion*, a prelude to the larger story of *The Lord of the Rings*, we meet a Creator named Eru Ilúvatar who fashions the universe with the help of mighty beings who bear a resemblance to biblical angels. Together, they use music to paint the cosmos and compose the overarching stories that will unfold within it.

One of the most powerful beings at Eru's side is named Melkor. Because of pride and jealousy, Melkor becomes the story's main adversary as he creates his own dark melody in an effort to taint Eru's symphony. A battle ensues, and eventually Eru takes what Melkor composed and turns it into something even more glorious than what was originally imagined.

This fictional tale, along with others like it, taps into eternal truths that we will explore more fully in the journey ahead. For now, the most important thing you need to know is that your life was always meant to be a song—one of awakened identity and joyful purpose. This song was dreamed up and set in a specific key long before you arrived here.

Somewhere along the way, however, the melody was stolen—locked away and hidden behind layers of fear, regret, and sorrow. The music of your identity and purpose became distorted. Static broke into the song of your true self, and the volume was turned way down on your calling to bear great gifts to the world.

And so we come to the purpose of this book. In the pages ahead, we will embark on an adventure to recover the key to that lost song. We will uncover ancient wisdom that leads us back home.

This is designed to be a **28-day journey**, offering a portion of truth each day to help re-tune the soul. But while it follows this daily rhythm, you are free to move at your own pace. Linger where you need to linger. Return to what stirs your heart. Skip ahead if something calls you forward.

The journey is arranged in four movements, much like a symphony. The **first movement** is a sacred scavenger hunt—a search for the divine key hidden in the harmonies of creation and scripture. The **second movement** brings us to the threshold, where we learn to place that key within the door of our inner life.

Then come the **final two movements**, where the key is turned and music begins to pour forth, awakening the deep song of the soul. This is where heaven collides with our everyday earthly lives and we step back into our truest self and highest calling.

Are you ready to tune in?

Let's begin.

Movement One

Treasure

Movement One

Day One: Revelation

God conceals the revelation of his word
in the hiding place of his glory.
But the honor of kings is revealed
by how they thoroughly search out
the deeper meaning of all that God says.
—Proverbs 25:2 TPT

There is a royal calling—a kingly quest—to which each of us is invited. It is the scavenger hunt of the ages, an adventure of the spirit that leads us to a treasure beyond anything found in the greatest works of fiction. This treasure is waiting for each one of us, calling to us from beyond the veil.

The treasure, very simply, is *revelation*.

But it's important to understand what revelation is—and what it isn't. It is *not* head knowledge. It is not merely a newfound fact. You can know things in your head that have little impact on your day-to-day life. For instance, a person might acknowledge that God exists and is full of love, yet that idea can remain only a vague thought, bearing no real influence on their emotional or spiritual life.

Revelation, on the other hand, involves a heart-awareness of truth. It is an unveiling of something so profound that it activates things deep within you, bringing about lasting transformation.

Another way to describe revelation is to compare it to a kind of heavenly currency that allows you to purchase spiritual riches. This isn't a perfect analogy, because the riches are already yours—they are freely available. But revelation is the inner awareness that enables you to realize the access you have to them.

Revelation is valuable beyond measure, and according to the wisdom of Solomon, the way to find it is within "his word." This is where our adventure begins. The word of God will be our treasure map to an absolutely life-changing revelation.

But what is his word? Many think the word of God refers to the holy scriptures:

God has transmitted his very substance into every Scripture, for it is God-breathed...
–2 Timothy 3:16a TPT

...and they would be right. Like the wooden manger that held the precious infant Christ, the scriptures—though made from the frail wood of humanity—hold divine wonders within. Accordingly, this is what most people think of when they hear the phrase "the word of God."

But there is more to the "word" than this. The treasure map we're unfolding is far more expansive, for it includes anything breathed forth by God's Spirit with divine purpose. This significantly enlarges our map, because we know God also breathed the cosmos into existence:

All he had to do was speak by his Spirit-Wind command,
and God created the heavenlies.
Filled with galaxies and stars,
the vast cosmos he wonderfully made.
–Psalm 33:6 TPT

Creation itself is a word from the Father. Indeed, there is *revelation-knowledge* hidden within its chambers:

Revelation

The heavens declare the glory of God;
And the firmament shows His handiwork.
Day unto day utters speech,
And night unto night reveals knowledge.
–Psalm 19:1-2 NKJV

But the map does not end here. Just as the scriptures and the stars received a special release of inspired breath from heaven, so did something else:

And the Lord God formed man of the dust of the ground, and breathed into his nostrils the breath of life; and man became a living being.
–Genesis 2:7 NKJV

Yes, you too are a *word* from heaven. Each of us was formed in our mother's womb by the same Spirit who fashioned gravity and wood. Within every human conception is a unique release of holy breath. Just as mysteries are hidden within the Bible and Creation, so too is there a mystery hidden within you. The unlocking of this mystery is the treasure of eternity, and it is the purpose of the journey upon which we now embark.

We are going to search for clues to this treasure in a variety of places touched by divine breath. To begin, we must travel very far from here—to the other side of the universe, to a galaxy (or multiple galaxies) far, far away.

Before we do, let us pause. This journey is long, and there is a blessing we will need activated in our hearts before we proceed. This blessing is found in the following words, written through divinely inspired breath. As you read them, receive them as though someone who really loves you—and has amazing faith—is praying them over you...

I pray that the Father of glory, the God of our Lord Jesus Christ, would impart to you the riches of the Spirit of wisdom and the Spirit of revelation to know him through your deepening intimacy with him.

I pray that the light of God will illuminate the eyes of your imagination, flooding you with light, until you experience the full revelation of the hope of his calling—that is, the wealth of God's glorious inheritances that he finds in us, his holy ones!
–Ephesians 1:17-18 TPT–

You are loved beyond imagination. Right now, take your stand against any orphaned thinking, any fearful voice that says there's never enough treasure to go around, or the nearsightedness that claims adventures with treasures at the end exist only in the movies—or, at best, in the sweet by-and-by after we die. Quiet down those biting interruptions and remember: you are loved and chosen.

There is treasure indeed, and you are invited to unlock its riches—for yourself, your family, and even for generations to come.

Day Two:
Strings

Our hunt begins at the furthest reaches of the cosmos with an image that flooded the news in the middle of 2022. I had just set my heart and pen to begin this book when the presidential office of the United States called a national press conference for the sole purpose of releasing a couple of photographs.

These pictures were the first images captured by NASA's James Webb Space Telescope. Released at this conference and then shared across millions of social media accounts, the inaugural photo captivated the nations. The enthusiasm and fanfare surrounding it were not exaggerated. There was a genuine excitement happening in the release of these pictures because they were touching something deep within the heart of humanity.

Telescopes such as the James Webb are designed to peer back as far as possible into the earliest moments of time. Upon its ridiculously expansive glass, particles of light that have been traveling across the entire known universe are captured and analyzed.

Like any regular camera, a telescope's lens captures light particles arriving from distant objects, allowing us to see where they came from. In the case of Webb, its infrared scopes can look through the veil of dust and darkness toward the universe's earliest moments.

Light that exploded long ago still radiates outward, and the James Webb captures those rays to produce images of the ancient past. Billions of dollars have been invested into instruments like this, all driven by a profound yearning to discover something about our own light-filled origin.

As you may know, this image is filled not with individual stars but with entire galaxies.[1] Each glowing point is an ocean of starlight, carrying titanic suns like bubbles of foam strewn across the sea—each bubble holding worlds upon worlds.

At the release of this photograph, astronomers stretched our imaginations even further by explaining just how much of the universe it actually captured. They noted that if you were to take a single grain of rice and hold it up at arm's length toward the sky, that tiny grain would cover the same portion of space shown in the image. (Read that again if you need to.) As immense as it is, this swirl of celestial oceans is only a fragment of what erupted from the breath of the Almighty.

---

1   NASA, ESA, CSA, and STScI. James Webb Space Telescope Deep Field. 2022. https://webbtelescope.org/.

Strings

Scientists devise instruments like Webb to study the endless pages of creation, the God-breathed word of the heavens. With glass and metal, they peer into the book of the universe, study its chapters of galaxies, read through paragraphs of stars, and dissect sentences of entire planets. They even examine the very grammar and syntax of creation by studying the particles that allow this mighty book to exist in the first place. But in the last century, scientists have sought to go even further. They've asked the question, *"What makes up the fabric of this divine word?"*

In other words, they've sought to understand the paper itself. This leads us to the next clue on our scavenger hunt.

The Music of the Cosmos

Some of our greatest minds have stumbled upon a beautiful possibility about the "paper" God uses to write his word upon. For now, these ideas remain in the realm of theory, for no combination of glass and metal can look that closely into creation. Nonetheless, supported by stunning mathematics, some scientists propose that at the foundation of everything lie one-dimensional "strings" from which all else is formed—including atoms and their constituent parts.

As each string is plucked, particular "notes" are played. These notes go on to give form, beauty, and substance to creation. The math behind this idea parallels the same mathematics governing violin strings. Fittingly, this concept has become known as string theory, though it has many other names and variations.

The theory suggests that all matter and forces are the result of vibrations playing upon the "strings" of the universe. Some mysterious force causes power to be released, moving these unimaginably small strings in different ways. Each movement then gives birth to different particles, which make up everything we see and experience.

Such an idea reframes our understanding of the treasure map of creation. It suggests that creation is more of a song sheet than a book. The One who breathed forth the cosmos really *sang it forth*. His word is music, and the spin of every galaxy is a dance.

Instruments like the James Webb Telescope are simply capturing some of creation's earliest "verses." By the time the galaxies in the preceding image formed, the opening notes had already commenced. The instruments were coming together to give structure and form to the larger music behind everything else. And thus, this was only the beginning of the song.

But something greater and more delightful was about to emerge. A chorus was coming—beautiful beyond comprehension, bigger than every galaxy put together. The meaning of this chorus will lead us to the life-changing treasure we seek.

As we proceed, please know that you do not need to understand physics or music theory to appreciate where we're headed. These insights are only clues from God's inspired treasure map of creation, pointing the way to something far greater than themselves.

And to find the next clue, we must journey to a completely different part of the map.

Day Three: Trinity

While scientists engineer devices to study the pages of creation, God has gifted us with people who make it their aim to study the pages of the written word of scripture. I had the opportunity to hang out with one such individual while speaking in a country that is quite hostile to the inspired words of scripture.

I was meeting with leaders from the underground church in an Asian nation, where people sing the songs of Jesus under the discord of a hostile government—somehow making their songs all the sweeter. There, a pastor friend unpacked something significant about the moment of creation. He took us a little further back than James Webb:

> *In the beginning God created the heavens and the earth. The earth was formless and void, and darkness was over the surface of the deep, and the Spirit of God was moving on the surface of the waters. Then God said, "Let there be light"; and there was light.*
> –Genesis 1:1-3

Hidden within these first three verses of the biblical text is a treasure of revelation regarding the One who sang forth the cosmos. Like many other mysteries in the Old Testament, we will require some special tools—particularly from the New Testament—to help us see it clearly.

In the book of John, we discover a kind of musical remix of Genesis 1. John starts at the beginning as well; however, he goes much further back than Genesis. He speaks of a relationship between Jesus Christ—who is called the "Word"—and the Father of creation.

> *In the beginning was the Word, and the Word was with God, and the Word was God.*
> –John 1:1

As the book progresses, John builds on this foundation by quoting specific lines from Jesus, in which he speaks of his oneness with the Father (John 10:30). Even in the painful hours leading up to his death, this union is put on display when we glimpse a conversation between Jesus and the Father, where Jesus speaks about the intimate connection they shared before anything else existed (John 17).

This union between Christ and the Father is scattered throughout other books of scripture. In other places we also see the Spirit of God functioning as a unique Person within this intimate relationship. Together, these passages reveal a wondrous treasure—the reality that God is Three-in-One. Father, Son, and Spirit.

This truth is strewn throughout the written word like stars in a galaxy. It is also written as a testimony within the universe itself. For example, consider the three essential things making up the fabric of our existence: time, matter, and space. Each has three distinct parts. Time consists of past, present, and future. Matter exists in three primary states: solid, liquid, and gas. Space is structured by three dimensions: height, width, and length. These three "trinities" of creation were birthed simultaneously at the dawn of the cosmos, all originating from the heart of a triune Creator.

Now if you're having a hard time seeing this truth hidden in Genesis 1, let me enlighten your search by highlighting three distinct parts:

Trinity

In the beginning <u>God</u> created the heavens and the earth. The earth was formless and void, and darkness was over the surface of the deep, and the <u>Spirit of God</u> was moving on the surface of the waters. Then <u>God said, "Let there be light"</u>; and there was light.
—Genesis 1:1-3

The easiest to identify here is God, the One who is the Father of creation, overseeing the making of heaven and earth. Amid this creative work, we also see the Spirit of God who is described as a distinct presence. But the most difficult to perceive is found in the third verse, when light bursts forth as God opens his mouth and speaks.

Song and Light

Here is where the New Testament helps us uncover the buried treasure. Back in the Gospel of John, Jesus is not only referred to as the Word of God but also as "the Light of the world" (John 8:12). Jesus is the very Substance through which the cosmos was made. As it says elsewhere, all creation was made *through him* (Colossians 1:16). Thus, in the first three verses of the Bible, we find a hidden picture of God the Father, God the Spirit, and God the Son co-creating the universe from an already established relationship. Incredible.

However, what we must come to terms with is that this co-creation was not some heavenly science project. It was not three highly intellectual entities drafting architectural designs and assembling particles in intricate patterns to display as some kind of trophy in heaven's library.

No. This was a joyful collaboration of song and light. The greater mystery is not merely that God is Three-in-One but that he is, as my friend Mo likes to say, "Three-in-Love." To uncover this truth in the map of the word, we must look at another passage from John's writings. He is the one who gifted us with this beautiful phrase:

"God is love..."
–1 John 4:8

...which leads us to stunning conclusions. Love, we know, is kind, hospitable, generous, and attentive. It puts the needs of others first. It is self-giving. Therefore, if God is love—and love exhibits these qualities—then there is much more to "God" than meets the eye. His very being is a deep, relational communion. And this is far beyond what the word "relationship" can convey. The Trinity was experiencing a joyful and dynamic interaction before the cosmic song sheet emerged. Their ecstatic communion of deep friendship and intimacy gave way to this massive building project.

So, to put it in other terms...the creation around us was sung and birthed by a *Divine Family*.

This truth is written into creation's songbook, for the reality of "family" pervades everything. Whether among human beings, the animal kingdom, plants, fungi, or even star systems—familial structures exist because of the One who set it all in motion. The perfect unity of the Trinity—diverse yet unimaginably cohesive—echoes throughout the universe.

An Unimaginable Dance

Many centuries ago, some of the early fathers and mothers of the faith coined a special term in an attempt to describe this triune mystery: *perichoresis*. This word paints a picture of a dancing circle. *Peri* is the root word of perimeter, while *choresis* relates to choreography. The term conveys the idea of God as *movement*—a circle of unending fellowship and joy.

Trinity

The mystery unveiled by Christ, the apostle John, and many others is that the Father, Spirit, and Son exist in a blissful relationship charged with unimaginable interaction. Within this circle of life-giving union is an adventurous friendship, and from this friendship flows the very rhythm by which the word—whether creation, scripture, or humanity—was inspired.

We are peering further back now, beyond the cosmic dust, and even beyond the singularity no telescope can capture. We are gazing into the face of a smiling, dancing God.

And we are surrounded not just by the word of God but by the *lyrics* of God. Thus, this is more than a song. Creation, scripture, and life itself are more like a ballad—a song and a story. This musical story grew like a burning dream within the heart of the Trinity, emerging from an already established rhythm. It was a song that each Person of the Trinity knew needed to be released.

This song is the focus of our journey. I tapped into it myself when I was worshiping with those Asian believers amid darkness and persecution. I could feel it all around me then. It is the song of awakened joy and the story of an inner freedom greater than any hostility around us.

We are drawing closer to the illuminating key that tunes us into this song and unlocks its full power. Let us continue with a few more thoughts from God's creation before merging them with other important clues found in scripture.

Day Four:
Quartet

The week before I headed to Asia, a friend gave my wife and me a gift. Knowing we would be away from each other for a while, they handed us a bunch of cash and told us to enjoy a night out. They said the Lord had prompted them to do so. Gratefully, we took the gift and decided to go on a boat ride in Manhattan.

As we drifted around the Statue of Liberty, a trio of jazz musicians played at the front of our vessel, providing an otherworldly night. We relaxed, soaked in the evening light, and watched three artists meld into one song. It was a magical time, enhanced by the atmosphere of jazz—a style of music with an uncanny ability to blend spontaneity and structure.

As I reflect on that evening, I'm reminded of how Jesus compared his Father to interesting individuals like farmers, businessmen, and judges. Following his lead, I'd like to go ahead and compare God to that jazz trio.

I tell you, the story of creation is like Three Musicians who, with joyful passion, brought forth one song with deep musical structure and quantum spontaneity. As this song poured out like breath from the Trinity's mouth, an incalculable number of vibrations went forth.

As we've learned, God laid out the sheet music of the cosmos and plucked the literal strings of creation to give form to everything around us. The universe is filled with design. Even the most atheistic theorists unwittingly acknowledge this when they describe our universe as "fine-tuned."

"Fine-tuned" is a widely used term throughout the scientific community to describe how perfectly aligned and precise the universe's properties are. Discoveries are being made all the time revealing how the slightest, most microscopic changes to the properties of atoms and their inner workings would cause the entire universe to collapse.

Our cosmos is fine-tuned because it has a very specific purpose. It is indeed a fine-tuned instrument, hand-crafted to play something of eternal significance…

The Coming of the Dream

When the Creator spoke and the harmonious cosmos took shape, the stage was set for a unique verse in the grand song of creation. Amid the billowing starscape, Earth emerged like an aqua diamond, shining in the sea of light. It was here that the Divine Family would prepare the way for the chorus of the song—a moment that would bring forth a personal, breath-like exhale, as if a soprano voice cut through the orchestral swell with crystal clarity or a saxophonist stepped into the spotlight, launching into a stunning jazz solo.

This solo was powerful beyond measure, yet it came as a still, small voice—a mere whisper in comparison to those first booming drums of creation. Here, the true meaning of the music began to emerge. It was the dream within the heart of the Creator coming into manifestation.

From the dust of this tiny planet came forth extremely special beings created by the Trinity. But not just *created*—oh, we must see this! A more appropriate term might be *birthed*. The classic clockmaker analogy falls woefully short in describing this moment. God wasn't merely constructing a complex piece of intricate clockwork. This was a Father releasing his seed—the very essence of his life—into the burgeoning creation.

Quartet

There upon that aqua jewel, the Holy Spirit hovered over the Father's seed, protecting and nurturing it like a mother's womb. This seed holds the purpose of our entire search through the treasure map of God's word. We've examined the word of creation and the word of scripture, each inspired and vocalized by God, but now we arrive at the moment where God sang out what everything else had been preparing the way for... The seed of human DNA.

This is our next major clue from the map of creation—what scientists call *deoxyribonucleic acid*.

DNA is remarkable. It's been compared to a written book, and for good reason. It's composed of a highly specific language, a code we're able to read and even rewrite with genetic technology. But to unite this with everything else we've learned, our DNA is not some informational bulletin. It is not a dull encyclopedia or some research document.

No—it is a songbook.

It is the pathway through which God captures the greatest part of his music.

Among the scientific community, there is universal agreement that this chemical substance would fall apart if even the slightest property of our finely tuned universe were altered. This is because it holds the meaning of the whole thing.

Yes, the very theme of the Trinity's heart dances up and down the spiraling staircase of their children's DNA. Human life is a doorway for heaven's love to invade this wildly precise instrument called the cosmos. In fact, it is the crown jewel—the chorus of the universe's music.

And so it turns out this singing Trinity was not only making music. They were preparing another musician to participate in their eternal glory.

That heavenly jazz trio was bringing forth a holy quartet.

Day Five:
Blessing

We are getting closer now. Our scavenger hunt through time, space, and scripture is leading to a glorious crescendo.

After the instruments of creation were set in place, the rhythm of its elements and forces flowing as one, the Creator breathed a much more personal "word" into this ensemble of energy and dust. What emerged were living beings, made from the same elements found in the stars surrounding them. Following this crowning exhale from God came the release of a "blessing" given to these newly born beings fashioned with the building blocks of DNA.

> *God blessed them; and God said to them, "Be fruitful and multiply..."*
> –Genesis 1:28

Many think this blessing was simply the command to "be fruitful and multiply." But that was actually a directive flowing out of the blessing itself. The book of Genesis does not record the precise words of God's blessing, either in this passage or when it is repeated in its 9th chapter.

There we find the earth covered by a famous flood, as a dove hovers over the waters—a sign that creation's song is being re-sung, like the *reprise* of a powerful chorus. When the waters subside, a small band of people emerge—Noah and his surviving family. To them, God releases the same blessing once more.

The words of the actual blessing remain concealed in the Old Testament. Much like the reality of God's triune nature, they are fully revealed only in the New. Let us continue then in our royal pursuit of revelation, for within this original blessing, we will discover the key that unlocks the treasure we seek.

Love an Aloha

Though the Gospel of Mark is not the first book in the New Testament, most scholars believe it was the earliest account of Jesus's life to be penned. In its opening chapter, we find the Father pouring out incredible words over his Son. In a hidden way, Genesis 1 plays itself out once more. It is another reprise.

To reiterate what we've been saying: the "chorus" of creation is humankind, the younger brothers and sisters of the eternal Son of God. In scripture, this chorus began with the creation of Adam. It played again with Noah, resurfaced in the lives of Joseph and David, and echoed throughout the lives of other biblical figures. But now, it returned with more power than ever. Now, the full measure of the song and the true nature of its theme were about to be revealed.

In Mark's opening scene, the Spirit is once again hovering over water. We see a dove descending upon the Jordan River as Jesus of Nazareth is baptized. Here, the Father, Son, and Spirit appear together once more, and the following words are released like a timeless solo from the Composer himself:

> *Then a voice came from heaven, "You are My beloved Son, in whom I am well pleased."*
> –Mark 1:11 NKJV

Here is the same verse from The Passion Translation:

> *At the same time, a voice spoke from heaven, saying: "You are my Son, my cherished one, and my greatest delight is in you!"*
> –Mark 1:11 TPT

Blessing

I'm also a fan of the Hawaiian Pidgin version:

An wow! Get one voice from da sky tell, "You my boy! I fo real kine get love an aloha fo you, an I stay good inside cuz a you!"
–Mark 1:11 HPB

Through the life of Jesus, we finally discover what was in that original blessing. Though he is completely divine, Jesus is 100% human—born from the same DNA spun out of creation's songbook. Because of his humanity, Jesus reveals the truth that had been spoken over his brothers and sisters from the very beginning. *This* was the blessing released upon Adam and Eve:

I love you.

You delight me so much.

You make me feel good inside.

You're mine!

As humanity opened the eyes of their consciousness for the first time, they would have immediately seen the sparkling gaze of a Father delighting over them. It would have also been the eyes of a Mother, dancing with gratitude over her creation.

For a moment, think of the implications here. When Adam was created, he was not given a to-do list. Nor was he told to grovel on the ground before his Maker. He was simply born into love and acceptance. And from that foundation, he was told to enjoy and beautify the world.

I remember the same feelings welling up in my heart as I held each of my daughters soon after they emerged from the darkness of the womb. In those precious moments, I wanted nothing from them. There was nothing they needed to do to earn my love. Love simply sprang from my chest, as though something deep in my own DNA was wired to feel this way. I just adored them. And smiled. And tears streamed down my face, like gentle doves descending on my cheeks.

This blessing—pictured in the Adam and Eve story, reprised throughout the Old Testament, and fully revealed in the words the Father spoke over the Son—was not meant to stay with Jesus alone. From the beginning, he desired to share the blessing with others. Thus, it is now sung over each and every one of us:

> *The Lord your God in your midst,*
> *The Mighty One, will save;*
> *He will rejoice over **you** with gladness,*
> *He will quiet **you** with His love,*
> *He will rejoice over **you** with singing.*
> –Zephaniah 3:17 NKJV

At the moment of every conception, there is the approving smile of a Father who knits us together with twirling threads of finely spun DNA. Over the womb of every woman bearing life, the Trinity sings words of pure delight.

This blessing—this "word," this song of bliss—brings forth the power to be fruitful and multiply. All of us are destined to be fruitful like our Creator, multiplying love and grace through the unique instrument of our lives. Indeed, we are co-musicians with the Trinity, called to play our own unique sound in the unfolding story of the cosmos.

As stated in the Prelude, we are searching for a key that unlocks the music within our souls. What we are discovering is that this key has everything to do with tuning in to the sound of God's original love for us. The core of our nature and the furthest reaches of our destiny converge in this blessing of acceptance and grace. This is our origin, and it is where we recover all that has been lost.

But we are not here for mere ideas and theory. We seek life-changing revelation. We long to tangibly grab hold of this reality and place it into the doorway of our hearts. And so, we will go deeper now into the scriptures, where we will discover the strange shape and form of this key.

Day Six:
Lightning

Beyond the veil of time, space, and scripture, deep in the happy home of the Trinity's heart, a celebratory dance was underway. Within this dance was a burning desire, a yearning to share their life with others.

To have children.

And so, God released the seed of his word. He spoke, and his Spirit moved like rain upon that seed. Humanity came forth from a universe that was carefully bent and crafted like the wood and strings of a masterful violin.

Into these little beings, the Trinity released a personal blast of life. Like a musician breathing into the mouth of a flute, God released into us the very force of life within himself. This breath came with a blessing of complete adoration and acceptance.

Another way to say this is that humanity was *kissed* into life. The Maker gave their blessing by leaning into Adam's dusty frame and releasing the personal touch of a kiss.

> *Then the Lord God formed man of dust from the ground, and breathed into his nostrils the breath of life; and man became a living being.*
> –Genesis 2:7

The key we seek, the answer to our soul's awakening, is this original blessing of the Spirit's grace.

The Kiss of Christ

But now we see how this blessing comes in the form of a kiss. This will be our final clue to the **X** on the treasure map.

If we were to continue our hunt for a similar message, we would eventually come to a place in the Bible that carries this same truth but in a clearer way. It is a musical poem that often gets neglected or misunderstood in the study and teaching of scripture. Yet its lyrics are buried like hidden jewels within the divine breath.

It opens like this:

> *The most amazing song of all, by King Solomon.*
> *Let him smother me with kisses—his Spirit-kiss divine...*
> –Song of Songs 1:1-2 TPT

A Divine Conduit

We talked about telescopes earlier. Let's discuss lightning rods for a moment.

Did you know a single bolt of lightning is five times hotter than the surface of the sun? It's an uncanny burst of power. Humankind has learned to redirect and even harness this power by erecting certain metals that attract the force of lightning and divert it into a safe place within the dust of the earth. Such rods are usually at the top of buildings, connected to metalwork that carries the power down to the building's foundations.

Over the millennia, there have been conduits of God that have collected the musical lightning swirling all around us. These conduits have been designed to bring this power into the dust and foundation of our being. Solomon's pen was one such instrument. His greatest work—the Song of Songs—was the result.

Lightning

Solomon begins his work by giving it an incredible designation. He proclaims that this is *the Song of all songs*. The assertion is that this is the most amazing, the most wonderful, the most remarkable Song ever written, in heaven or on earth (which would include the untold angelic ballads in the heavenly realms). It is the Song of the Ages.

I believe every good song taps into the original one that birthed creation. It is an inner echo of that first ballad that makes all good music truly good. Even sad songs, with their minor chords, contribute to the ache and yearning for that greater song's "major" completion.

That said, I want to build the case that Solomon's Song, more than any other, taps into the fullness of this original music, giving us its richest volume. This includes not only the glorious chorus of humanity we've been discussing but also a breathtaking finale. For that reason, the Song will give great illumination into the DNA within us. More than that, we will find that it unlocks our deepest potential—our true identity and highest destiny. It starts with a desire for the kiss of original blessing and then teaches us how to receive it.

One of the great teachers of Israel, Rabbi Akiva, often referred to as "the chief of the sages," once said that the entire universe is unworthy of the day the Song of Songs was given to Israel. He called it the "holy of holies" of scripture. We will see that it is a place where life, creation, and scripture collide, leading to an explosion of transformative truth.

Solomon's Song is the sound of heaven distilled into eight chapters of ancient poetry. As its light gets channeled through the pen of a wise king, its transcendent power remains hidden beneath the sometimes-awkward wrapping paper of romantic poetry. This treasure is further concealed within the larger collection of writings known as the Old Testament. But now, it is the glory of God's rising kings to uncover its depths. For in this Song of all songs, we find that creation is going somewhere—and each of us is called to be a co-musician in the symphony.

Keep in mind, the larger song of creation carries lyrics with a very specific theme. The sheet music of creation was only a rhythmic backdrop for the emergence of image-bearers. But even that was just the beginning of something far grander than we can imagine.

This revelation is beyond our ability to bear. A thousand lightning strikes upon the human body would fall short of describing the weight of its lyrics. But thankfully, the poetry of Solomon provides a type of instrumentation that can safely carry it into your dusty frame and reinvigorate you with eternal life.

Indeed, the "metal" that this divine Song is wrapped around is composed of romantic metaphors. Countless theologians and spiritual leaders over the centuries have taken the outer wrappings of this Song and turned it into a text on human marriage and relationships. There is truth to this, but it misses the real point.

In the Song of Solomon, we find passages about a woman longing to be with her beloved and the beloved swooning over the beauty of his bride. When we read these things, we find a deep mystery pointing us to something beyond our imagination. It all speaks to an immense love from God toward the human soul and how receiving that love can change everything.

Sadly, many are uncomfortable with the book's themes. This is especially true of those who have a hard time embracing the romantic nature of God's heart. With minds buried in super-spiritual clouds or fearful images of the Divine, many miss the romance and beauty infused within creation itself.

Lightning

A cosmic judge with a long white beard and a stoic face did not create sunsets and wine. These things were made by the hand of a divine Lover and Friend. Creation is the overflow of a romantic heart, a God passionately in love with the ones for whom this music was made.

And speaking of judges, there are many who prefer to describe the "Gospel of Jesus" as a courtroom drama rather than a beautiful epic. But the Gospel—the Good News of what happened in the life, death, and resurrection of Jesus—is the real story and Song of the Trinity's heart. It is not about a courtroom but a captivated Bridegroom who would stop at nothing to have his beloved enter into the fullness of the music within her. Solomon's symbolic poetry will help us see this beautiful Gospel like never before.

Ultimately, the Song will show us that the Gospel is a kiss, and this kiss is the key that unlocks the treasure deep inside our own inspired being.

Day Seven:
Kiss

I remember kissing my wife for the first time—the rush of fluttering in the heart, the weakening of the knees. And, of course, the awakening of certain energies, a reason for which I tell young people to be careful about whom they lay their lips on before marriage. There's a magic in that connection as two puzzle pieces hardwired with a chemical cocktail intersect. Romantic kissing very quickly leads to other things because it's designed to be an initiating force into life—as in reproduction. Indeed, a kiss is a key that can unlock the life force of our being.

Now, we're obviously talking about the chemistry of our bodies, but there's a deeper chemistry in the soul we're going to uncover. Our soul was made to be kissed as well. There is a divine kiss that awakens us to the true substance of life, causing us to be "fruitful" in the deepest sense of the word. But this kiss can only come from one true Source.

One true Lover.

The Song of Songs begins with a cry for this divine kiss. It is spoken by a woman whom King Solomon fell for. Solomon was a real king in a real nation some 3,000 years ago who was likely smitten by a young shepherdess in a region of his kingdom called Shulam. This "Shulamite" lady took his breath away, and he responded by writing poetry about her (a good outlet when the logical part of the brain can't do justice in expressing what's happening in the heart).

But let's be clear. This historical context (which may not even be completely accurate) is only thin wrapping paper covering the treasure inside. And it's actually somewhat crude wrapping paper when you consider Solomon's natural life, particularly his polygamy. Nonetheless, God has a way of redeeming human brokenness and hiding glory even in the most unseemly places.

What we'll find is that this woman represents each of us. Solomon, then, represents the One who would fall to earth to pursue and rescue our hearts.

After the Song gives its opening title and proclamation, the next verse goes like this:

> *Let him kiss me with the kisses of his mouth—*
> *For your love is better than wine.*
> —Song 1:2 NKJV

Within these words—*the kisses of his mouth*—is that same hidden picture of the Trinity we discussed earlier in Genesis 1. Look at it again with three words underlined:

> *Let <u>him</u> kiss me with the <u>kisses</u> of his <u>mouth</u>*
> *For your love is better than wine.*

Once again, we are *reprising* truths originally sung out in Genesis. The subject here is God. The Shulamite is calling out to the One who created her, the One who knows the way back to true life—God the Father. But she is specifically calling for the "kisses" of his mouth, which points us to his breath—God the Spirit. This is the same breath that turned Adam into a living being and now knits together all his descendants in their mothers' wombs.

She goes on to compare this kiss to wine, further establishing a connection to the Holy Spirit. Throughout the treasure map of scripture, wine is a clear symbol for the Spirit. Take, for instance, when Jesus's church was birthed at Pentecost. His apostles were accused of being drunk on "new wine" when, in fact, they were experiencing the overflow of the Spirit in their hearts (Acts 2:13). In another book of the Bible, a different apostle contrasts natural wine with the wine of the Spirit (Ephesians 5:18). There are other connections, but we'll leave it there.

So, we have here a hidden reference to both the Father and the Spirit. Where then is the Son?

He is found in the word *mouth*.

The mouth is the vessel through which a "word" comes forth. Jesus is the Word who releases the kiss of the Spirit, all of which comes from the heart of our Father. Thus, these first few verses of the Song are re-singing the first few verses of Genesis. Father, Son, and Spirit are found creating humanity once again.

Hidden Fires

To some degree, this young woman from Shulam knows this kiss is where she truly comes from. She knows something about how it birthed life itself when it pressed into earthen clay and transformed the dust into a living being. She wants to experience this kiss that birthed an advanced civilization on a rocky sphere and ignited an advancing church in the book of Acts. She desires this kiss above all else—which is why she represents all humanity.

People everywhere are hungering for love's true kiss. This spark of desire gets misdirected all the time into broken relationships, addictions, affairs, pornography, and much more. But no kiss will ever satisfy the deeper yearning of the soul.

The loving breath of God upon our inner being is what produces true life. Everything else is called "religion" and "philosophy." Such things carry great ideas that can titillate the mind and inspire different degrees of devotion, but they can do nothing to awaken the hidden fires of the soul. Because of this, the Shulamite speaks to everyone who is on a collision course with destiny, including every person who is not content to stay in dead, dry religion.

Our brief scavenger hunt has brought us to this revelation. When God released their blessing, it came on the heels of divine breath. Our original blessing *was* a divine kiss. And thus, this kiss of God, received in the heart, is what produces true fruitfulness and multiplication of life. In fact, there is no life apart from this Spirit-kiss.

It's also important to note that after the Shulamite prays for this kiss, she gives a follow-up request: *"Draw me after you and let us run together"* (v. 4). This will become clearer at the end of our journey, but for now, we will just highlight that within her heart is also the call to "run" with her Creator. In other words, she knows she carries a calling to run to the nations with the message of God's love. This can only happen, however, as she receives the divine spark for herself.

This kiss of Christ is the secret chord that unlocks the depths of our own being. It also opens up the meaning of creation's music. Even the words of what we call the "Holy Bible" are unveiled by its power. Everything in life, creation, and scripture coincides with this opening prayer of the Shulamite. Therefore, it is truly the **X** on our inspired treasure map.

Yet our journey is just beginning. Now we must start digging into the soil of the text, for there is life-changing revelation that follows this prayer. The entire book of Solomon's Song is about the Shulamite learning to receive this kiss. The poem then shows the fullness of her being consumed by the transforming breath of God.

You, beloved reader, are invited into a songful journey of being kissed as well. This is the key that opens the door to the greatest treasure imaginable. For here is the last thing to know as we start to dig: *You are the **X** on the treasure map as well.*

You are a carrier of glory, knit together with divine DNA and made to experience an indescribable adventure of intimacy and purpose.

Your Abba Father and his Son, Jesus, our Bridegroom King, want to release the Spirit of affirmation upon your own heart. Your call is only to hear it and receive it—to let it enter your believing soul and be gently turned within.

SELAH

Before we go further, we have need of a pause. Let's take a moment to reflect, using a special word often employed by the father of the one who wrote the Song of Songs—King David.

Selah is a musical term that appears many times in the book of the Psalms. While its exact meaning remains uncertain, it is typically associated with a kind of pause or a moment of recollection. Most likely, it signifies a kind of interlude—a time to come away from the logical ideas in a song or prayer and simply *be*.

Some scholars believe this term was included in these ancient songs because musicians of the time needed to re-tune their strings while playing. The lyres and harps that accompanied much of David's music could easily fall out of tune, and a *selah* provided a moment to bring the instruments back to their proper sound—literally, to a pleasing vibration, which is what musical notes are.

This concept beautifully mirrors our journey. All of us have, in some way, broken communion with the perfect sound of grace—the *pleasing* notes that resonate when we hear our Father declare our true and original blessing: *I am so pleased with you!*

The strings of creation find their highest order in human beings, yet we have lost their correct tuning. This discord is something we will unravel as we follow in the footsteps of the one called the Shulamite.

Ultimately, this journey is about returning to harmony. The entire Song is a divine *selah*, a holy pause. It is a "sabbath" for your very DNA—a reset that brings you back in tune with the music and kiss of your Creator.

So take a moment now and breathe.

Inhale. As you do, imagine taking in the very breath of God, swirling all around you. Envision it coursing through your blood, remaining within you even as you breathe out.

Exhale. Release the kiss of your breath back to him. As you do, ask for more revelation. Ask for love's true kiss to overtake your heart.

Then, allow him to speak.

Listen.

Do this often as you journey through this Song of the Ages…

In fact, as you go into the next three movements, consider stepping away for your own personal *selah* at the end of each chapter—or whenever something strikes your heart in a deeper, weightier way. You can even set a timer for 5, 10, or 20 minutes to help you lose yourself in the moment.

But whenever you pause, believe that God is right there with you. As you breathe and reflect on whatever is touching your heart, trust that he will meet you there. He will take delight in showing you more. So in those moments, watch what comes to your heart and mind. Consider writing it down and turning it into a deeper conversation.

And with that—let's move forward.

Movement Two

Discord

Day Eight:
Broken Identity

In the Prelude to this book, we discussed the origin story of J.R.R. Tolkien's *The Lord of the Rings*, where a Creator named Eru Ilúvatar fashions the story of creation with music. This, however, gets disrupted when other forces bring disharmony into the song.

This fictional story, penned well after the Song of Songs (though slightly before the development of string theory), parallels many things we've learned. It paints a vivid picture of the reason behind the evils of this world. There is a distortion in the original "music" of creation. Whether it's war, hunger, suicide, or depression, a dark melody is interrupting the rhythms we were meant to live by.

As we progress through the ancient poetry of Solomon, we'll come to understand that this battle is between the false sound and the true. We are in the midst of a cosmic tension, and this tension manifests itself even in the literal music we create.

A good jazz song, for instance, is built with a tension that eventually gives way to release. The human ear is designed to synchronize with this wrestling match between tension and release. This is because the journey of life itself is bound within this same dynamic.

The tension we will find in Solomon's Song is between separation and union. One is false; the other is true. But while the false is built on lies, it still strikes us as a seemingly real experience. Thus, the journey of the Shulamite is an adventure back into the true sound of union and grace.

Two Trees

Before we go forward, let's first go back to Genesis. In Genesis 1, we found our original blessing of love and the call to live from the "sound" of this blessing. We saw how we were designed to live, breathe, and move within the acceptance of our Creator and the truth that we are his delightful reflection. This truth was meant to be a life-giving tree producing the fruits of love, joy, and peace in our lives. The Tree of Life found in Genesis 2 points to this reality.

Genesis 3, however, is where tension comes in and the music gets distorted. It is there we see a lying serpent whispering a demonic lullaby into the ears of humanity. His smooth lyrics are along these lines:

There is another tree, and if you eat from it, you will become like God.

In this moment, something tragic unfolds. Eve, a daughter of the Trinity, listens to the serpent and loses sight of her true reflection. Fear sweeps in. Shame rides along with it. Discordant notes and minor keys. A step away from harmony, with more steps to come. The symphony changes. The vibrant music that was meant to produce a dance of joyful grace is transfigured into a dirge of gloom. This is where "sin" enters the picture, which simply means the dance of life became awkward and jittery.

And it all happened because we bit into a lie.

But what was the lie? It is hidden subtly beneath the suggestion: *If you do this ("eat from this tree"), you will be like God.*

The insinuation here is that Eve was not *already* like God—that she wasn't his image and likeness, declared as very good. Instead, she was now missing something.

Broken Identity

Yet all of this was a contradiction to the original sound of blessing that had been spoken into her soul like a kiss on the heart.

Thus, this initial deception was like a false kiss that brought death instead of life. We could also describe it as a broken key that brought her out of tune with reality. By eating and receiving this lie, she rejected God's word and began to doubt his heart. Trust, the very currency of relationship, was broken. Through it all, Eve lost sight of both her Father and herself.

In the Song of Songs, we see this same narrative play out through the character of the Shulamite. After the first verses subtly introduce the Trinity and their life-giving breath, we are then ushered into a series of discordant notes that come to steal the music:

> *I am dark, but lovely*
> *O daughters of Jerusalem*
> *Like the tents of Kedar,*
> *Like the curtains of Solomon.*
> –Song 1:5 NKJV

There are two ways to read this verse. On one level, it speaks to a confusion over who she is. She describes herself as both dark and lovely. In other words, both good and evil.

The tents of Kedar she mentions were the cracked desert dwellings used by a nomadic tribe descended from Ishmael. Ishmael was a son of Abraham who, in the New Testament, comes to represent unbelief and sin (Galatians 4:21-31). But then she equates herself to the curtains of Solomon, the linen hangings within the Holy Place of God's temple. This is a clear metaphor for beauty and holiness, as she compares herself to the very objects enfolding God's glory in the center of Solomon's famous temple.

And so, we find a fractured self-image. A wild tension. No longer is she looking into the pure reflection of the Trinity but rather a kind of distorted carnival mirror. She sees the good but identifies with darkness at the same time. As a result, her identity is twisted. She has eaten a false understanding, a *gnosis* of untrue melodies that now strum upon the instrument of her soul.

In other words, she has eaten from the Tree of the Knowledge of Good and Evil.

I am lovely. And I am dark. I am good. And I am bad.

The Shulamite's eyes have shifted into a perspective of *dualism*. There are layers of meaning to this term, but in this context, I'm referring to a two-sided identity where we see ourselves (and God) as both good and evil.

Such a vision is what originally produced the twin fruits of guilt and fear. We see this further in the Genesis narrative when Adam and Eve hide among the bushes after hearing the sound of the Trinity calling out to them. This broken vision caused them to fear their Creator, leading to all kinds of distorted ideas about his heart and nature. Ultimately, it led to an even deeper sense of separation.

But with this came an unquenchable desire for reconnection. We continued to seek after union in so many ways, though nothing satisfied. The seeds of deception produced a harvest of burdensome religions and philosophies. As the children of Eve traveled east of Eden, humanity forged countless paths of physical, mental, and spiritual strategies to escape our supposedly evil existence. But to use a modern expression, these escape plans became a "carrot on a stick" that we could never quite attain.

The desperation for renewed innocence remained intense—so intense that we would go as far as killing ourselves and others to find it. Yes, the false kiss (*I am dark*) even spawned the sacrifice of animals and young children. This is because innocent beings were thought to possess a purity that could be transferred to the guilty through sacrifice. Yet all of it was a terrible and failing effort to cleanse the soul of its discord.

In all of this, we lost sight of our Creator's original kiss of truth…

You are my beloved child, hewn from my own DNA.

And you still bring me the greatest delight.

Listen Closely…

There is a second way to read this passage—one that requires us to tune our ears and listen closely for the sound of Another. For there is actually a hidden dialogue happening here.

Since the ancient manuscripts of the Song of Songs do not delineate between speakers, translators must guess where to insert the speakers' names. This is not a perfect science, for it leaves much to interpretation. In this case, the Shulamite could be saying, "I am dark," but then a reply comes from the One she will see as her Shepherd and King. He responds with the opposite reality.

You are lovely.

She then says: *But my life is like the cracked tents of Kedar!*

And he speaks back: **You are like the fine linen curtains surrounding the very glory of God in my temple.**

The Kiss of Christ

Here we see the Lord answering her cry for a kiss. Yes, the kiss and key of his word are already coming upon her. But unfortunately, something is blocking it from penetrating and unlocking what lies within. Next, we'll look at how this blockage is humanity's deepest enemy and the main thing we're called to overcome.

Day Nine: Religion's Song

When humanity swallowed the seeds of deception, allowing bitter notes and twisted lyrics to take root within, the result was a demonic melody of fear playing through our collective souls. Suddenly, verses of destruction and stanzas of death were brought into the world. The original song of creation—with DNA as its greatest instrument—quickly became corrupted.

In this next verse, we see the effects of this problem as the Shulamite responds to God's kiss with rejection. Yet again, the Genesis story is being remixed. Like Adam and Eve, the Shulamite hides in the bushes of shame, the sound of fear blocking her ability to discern the Voice of Love.

> *Do not stare at me because I am dark,*
> *because I am darkened by the sun.*
> *My mother's sons were angry with me*
> *and made me take care of the vineyards;*
> *my own vineyard I had to neglect.*
> –Song 1:6 NIV

She declares once more that she is "dark" and attributes it to the heat of the sun. Typically, the sun is a good symbol, as it points to the light of God. Here, however, we find that her work under the sun's glory has caused darkness to grow in her life. This happened, she says, as she worked out in the vineyards of her mother's sons…

Beginning to Dig

Now would be a good time to pause and get our bearings, recalling what we've learned thus far. God's word is a treasure map leading to *revelation*, the hidden currency of heaven that unlocks our destiny and inheritance.

God's "word" encompasses all creation and all scripture. As we've searched this larger map of the word, we found the Song of Songs to be a key place holding its highest treasures. It is our **X** on the map, and so now we must start digging through the book's symbols in order to tap into its riches. This means figuring out what the people and objects in the poem represent.

We already know the Shulamite symbolizes humanity and the King is a metaphor for God. The sought-after kiss represents the truth of God's deep and affirming love for us. The kiss is also the Spirit of truth, for the Spirit releases into our hearts the blessing of our beloved identity (Romans 8:15-16).

Now we come to another symbol in the story—the mother. To interpret its meaning, we will pull back and look again at the larger map of scripture. We don't want to be like some who pull allegorical meanings out of their hat as they claim divine revelation. Instead, we will utilize other parts of the map to witness and testify to each symbol's unique meaning.

Thankfully, it doesn't take much Bible knowledge to figure this one out. There are three overlapping ways to understand the mother. In the New Testament, the redeemed people of God, both Jew and Gentile, are compared to a mother (see Galatians 4:26). In this way, the larger body of people known as the "church" is the mother of the Song.

However, we can go back further into scripture and see how the mother image relates directly to the nation of Israel. It was from the womb of Israel that the church was "birthed."

But we can go back even further to find the mother relating to the one who is literally called *mother of all the living*—Eve.

Putting this all together, we find the mother represents the family of God. Hence, working out in the vineyards can represent the place of serving God and his people.

But it is in this part of the Song where we find the Shulamite is burnt out—literally. She's engaged in good works but to the neglect of her own soul's flourishing. This speaks to religious labor, whether Christian, Jewish, or the many religious expressions that Eve's sons (her "mother's sons") have laid upon the backs of those seeking inner peace. This continues to parallel the Genesis narrative and the idea of man's religious efforts being birthed at the Tree of Knowledge.

Obviously, we're not referring to the pure kind of religion where we care for the marginalized and abandoned, treating them according to their original blessing in the Father (James 1:27). Rather, this is a religion built on those first lies of separation and fear. It speaks to the larger systems of guilt influencing all Abrahamic religions, as well as those that went further east, setting people on a broken path to fix a broken identity.

In one form or another, the spiritual systems of this world hold to a belief in an inner darkness that is a seemingly undefeatable force. All of them, even parts of religious Christianity, put people on a quest to "die to self," teaching that death is the only path to find freedom (whether metaphorically or literally). No matter what walk of life we come from, all of us have found ourselves impacted by this belief system, and it drives us into a place of striving for relief from this darkness.

The Shulamite is weary of all this striving, and so she cries out to her Creator. Though she's still blinded to the kiss of truth being offered to her, she knows enough to ask for more help.

> *Won't you tell me, lover of my soul,*
> *where do you feed your flock?*
> *Where do you lead your beloved ones*
> *to rest in the heat of the day? ...*
> –Song 1:7 TPT

So great is her desire for true rest. The Shulamite longs to return to the words of Genesis 1, where we were called "very good." This was the seventh day of creation, which came right after we were quickened to life and met with eyes of complete acceptance and delight.

But *what must I do?* is her question. What "work" does it take to get back there? What self-help module do I need to follow? What mantra or discipline of the mind must I manifest in order to find this return?

Such are the questions on the heart of a very tired human race.

Wanting rest but not knowing the way to find it, the Shulamite makes quite the illuminating statement. The following words will unlock another level of revelation as we dig deeper into this heavenly storehouse.

She says this:

> *...Why should I be like a veiled woman*
> *as I wander among the flocks of your shepherds?*
> –Song 1:7 TPT

Day Ten:
The Harlot

Some years after my trip to Asia, I returned to a different country to meet up with a group of people carrying a vision to see God's original blessing reawakened in that same part of the world. For all the beauty of this continent, a giant stain is smeared across its terrain in the form of human trafficking. It is one of the great distortions of life's original melody, reaching its loudest volume in places that embrace a low view of humanity. Its tentacles certainly touch the whole world, but the nations steeped in the most ancient forms of dualism seem to attract its viral touch the most.

A big part of the trip involved dealing with resistance in the atmosphere to the true music of grace. We call this intercession. Our focus was to prepare the ground of people's hearts to receive the hope-filled message that others would be trained to bring to them over the coming months and years.

One of our prayer assignments involved a walk through the local red-light district. While there, I passed by a young woman who was sitting directly across from her pimp, presenting herself to all who passed by. As I walked through this broken archway of the trafficked and trafficker, I caught eyes with the woman and saw a heartbreaking glimmer of fear hiding behind her gaze.

Today, in places like this, women are presented openly, scantily dressed. Yet in the days of Solomon, a woman would put a veil over her face as the advertisement for her services. This is why the Shulamite says she doesn't want to be like "a veiled woman wandering among the flocks." Many commentators believe she is comparing her current position to that of an ancient prostitute who covered her face and wandered through city streets in search of clients.

It's of great importance that we discuss this symbol of the veiled woman, for it unlocks our deepest problem. It also sets the course for the Shulamite to overcome what's blocking the kiss of God from reaching the depths of her being.

Mystery of the Harlot

First of all, a person's face speaks to their identity. From the shape and color of the eyes to the finer details of the complexion, the face sets us apart from everyone else. A dark veil covering someone's face is thus a picture of the true self being hidden behind deception.

But the meaning of this symbol comes into full bloom when we consider what prostitution is. A prostitute is someone who engages in an act of "love" through payment. A union occurs but only by way of paying for it—or earning it.

In other words, it's a metaphor for the broken and religious ways of man. Like paying a prostitute for an experience that's meant to come through a covenant of love, religion tries to buy its way into union. This is due to those initial lies that blinded (veiled) our eyes from seeing the union and fellowship we *already* shared with God. As we desperately tried to secure this original blessing through our own strength, the harlotry of self-effort grew throughout humanity. This is what we're finding in the image of a veiled woman striving out in the vineyards.

Now think about a vineyard for a moment. This is a place where the main ingredient for wine is produced. Earlier we learned that wine represents the very life of God—the Holy Spirit. It is particularly a symbol of the love, joy, and peace that flow from

God's heart. The veiled woman, burned out in the vineyards, is striving to find these things through her own efforts.

She could be speaking to those who are out seeking love through broken relationships and various sexual pursuits. She could be the person using drugs and other substances to find a fleeting sensation of joy. She could also be someone trying to create a sense of inner peace by accumulating enough money and power to insulate themselves from outward fears. No matter the circumstance, these pursuits all communicate how we have prostituted our souls in an effort to secure the true life and blessing of God.

The Shulamite has tasted and seen the emptiness of spiritual prostitution. As a result, she doesn't want to wander like such a woman "among the flocks." Flocks of sheep speak to the many gatherings of people in all kinds of spiritual pursuits. This reminds us that the "wandering" is not just a stroll down the pathways of sex, drugs, money, and power. Those are offshoots of an even broader path called religion.

But the Shulamite no longer wants to pursue union and acceptance by wandering around and paying for it with her own blood, sweat, and tears. Instead, she wants to find rest from the heat of her labor. She is looking for true peace.

And though she doesn't understand it yet, she is also searching for the true meaning of her name…

Two Names Intertwined

In the footnotes of The Passion Translation, there is a powerful insight regarding the names of the two main characters of the story—the Shulamite and King Solomon. Incredibly, these two names come from the same root word. It is the Hebrew term for peace, perfection, and wholeness.

Shalom.

And there's more to this, for "Shulamite" is the feminine version of this root word. "Solomon" on the other hand is masculine. This is significant because throughout scripture the human soul—which the Shulamite represents—is referred to with feminine language. Meanwhile, God is mostly referred to with masculine verbiage.

Obviously, male and female are both contained within humanity and within God. However, there's something about the human soul that specifically corresponds to God like female to male. The "female" representation of humanity and the "male" representation of God describe a mystery higher and more beautiful than any of our social orders or understandings of gender.

We are the Lord's *soulmate* in the truest definition of that term. We come from God and are made to return to him, like the depiction in Genesis where Eve is created out of the depths of Adam but then returns to him in covenantal love as a life partner.

So let's take a moment to tie this together. In the story, the Shulamite is at first a picture of the veiled human race. She is a symbol of all the world's engagements with false forms of love, where we wander in pointless efforts at attaining divine union. Because of this, the Shulamite not only represents the human soul; she specifically showcases the soul's journey of being *unveiled.*

But this unveiling leads us to another biblical symbol, one that is the exact opposite of a prostitute. One that speaks to humanity's true and original face.

A bride.

The Harlot

This is the biblical symbol for a union of the most pure and complete kind—the union we enjoyed at the start of our creation. Prostitution, on the other hand, is about pursuing what marriage was meant to give, yet seeking to attain it through paying clients who leave the next day.

In today's world, the prostitute's veil is our number one problem. Whether in small breakdowns of relationships or entire industries of literal sex trafficking, this veil works as a locked door over the minds of humanity, keeping us in dead-end paths of false relief and temporary pleasure.

Amazingly, when we pull back and look at the crescendo of the entire Bible, everything leads to the opposing imagery of these two different women—a prostitute and a bride (see Revelation 17-22). There we learn that the larger word of creation is building toward a great conflict between these realities, one of which will be burned with everlasting fire while the other will shine down through endless ages.

Yes, there is fire that can and will burn away this veil from the human race. It is both a kiss and a key, and it splits the veil in two and unlocks the door of our souls.

This is what the Shulamite is being ushered into, even though there is an inner resistance from those lies that stem all the way back to the Tree of Knowledge. She is being called to escape the dark melody of religion and retune her heart—"repent," you might say—to the music of grace.

Thankfully, the King will help her receive this kiss.

And he will do it by leading her to the only place where its power can be fully experienced.

Day Eleven: The Table

As we embark on this royal calling to dig through God's word and unearth its treasures, a surprising twist has come. We've discovered early on that the answer to everything our souls seek already lies within. And yet there is something blocking our ability to tap into it: a veil—dark, cold, and ancient—remains plastered over the mind.

And this veil requires a reckoning.

This reckoning, however, is not one of destructive wrath—at least not in the way people have typically understood such terms. The reckoning needed for this veil comes in a strange and unique form ... a kiss.

Yes, the world of fairy tales witnesses to a greater reality. It turns out that true love's kiss is what breaks the spell of a heavy sleep covering the eyes of humanity.

We will now follow the Shulamite on her own journey of waking up as she learns to receive this divine kiss for herself. At the beginning of the journey, she's learning to listen to the voice of God. She's starting to follow the Good Shepherd and his first set of instructions involves bringing her to another strange place.

Before we get there though, let's look at the word of advice he gives to her at the onset of the journey:

"Follow in the footsteps of the flock, and feed your little goats," says this Shepherd King (Song 1:8 NKJV).

Right away, God gives an encouragement to stay connected with a spiritual community and to continue looking for ways to care for those around her. Oftentimes, the wisdom we seek comes in the midst of community and service. Though a religious element needs to be burned away from her life, the Lord does not call the Shulamite to abandon all forms of connection with the "flocks" around her. Such words are reminiscent of something found much later in scripture:

And let us consider how to stimulate one another to love and good deeds, not forsaking our own assembling together, as is the habit of some, but encouraging one another; and all the more as you see the day drawing near.
—Hebrews 10:24-25

With this word of wisdom established, she is then ushered into the only place where freedom is found:

As the king surrounded me at his table,
the sweet fragrance of spikenard
awakened the night.
—Song 1:12 TPT

The Shepherd King has led her to a table—his table.

Now, if this King truly represents Jesus, the one who is also called the Lamb of God, then there is only one way to understand this next symbol: it is the table of the Lamb.

Or, as many refer to it, *the communion table*.

This is the place where we encounter the greatest expression of love to ever appear on the earth.

The Table

The Release of Divine Blood

Most readers will be familiar with the act of communion, where bread and wine are administered in some form or another—the bread as Jesus's broken body, the wine his shed blood. As we eat, we are partaking of a mystery that culminated on a Roman cross two thousand years ago. There, Jesus Christ was crucified, pouring out his blood to secure what the apostle Paul called "our redemption" (Colossians 1:14).

Consider something for a moment. The foundation of human blood is the substance we discussed earlier: DNA. Our finely tuned universe allows this remarkable spiraling ladder of life to exist. It turns out this substance is a bridge between heaven and earth, for the Creator literally stepped down this ladder to enter the physical realm. God the Son took on human flesh in the person of Jesus of Nazareth.

Jesus was woven together in the womb of a Jewish girl named Mary. He was born with a beating heart, just like the rest of us, and with breath in his lungs, he went on to tell his followers that he was giving his life for the world (Mark 10:45). Speaking to people who were familiar with the ancient words of Moses, they would know the reality that "life is in the blood" (Leviticus 17:11).

Communion brings us back to the moment when Jesus completed this act, pouring out the pinnacle of creation—DNA—on the soil of our planet. He did this to rescue us and bring us back to the original music of creation. In this way, his death became a gateway into life.

This, of course, isn't all that strange when we go back to the testimony of God's creation. Our breath and DNA are only possible because of elements born from the violent death of stars. In the wake of their explosion, the elements necessary for life emerge. In the same way, the death of the Son releases what is necessary for us to experience true life—everlasting life.

And this is what the Bible calls an act of redemption, an old term that typically meant buying something back. Something that once belonged to you could be redeemed, but only if you paid the proper price. In biblical times (and still today), something could only be redeemed with something else of like value. You couldn't use a couple of shekels to redeem an entire plot of land that once belonged to your family. You had to pay the full price of that property to get it back.

Jesus's apostles declared that Jesus paid the full price of our redemption by pouring out his blood. This unveils something astounding about humanity and the blood coursing through our own veins. Our redemption price was the sacred DNA of God himself!

Just pause and take that in. This means we are of *like value* to God …

In other words, Jesus's blood reveals the divine value of our lives. This is one glorious aspect of his death: that Christ poured out his DNA to reveal and redeem our true selves.

However, there is something else. Jesus's death was described as a demonstration (Romans 5:6-8). He specifically demonstrated a love for us that was bigger than our raging unbelief and rebellion.

In his coming, Jesus took on the full brunt of human deception. He stood against the height of wickedness as he faced the twin forces of man's religion and politics. He took these things on, absorbing the full wrath of their attack with open arms of mercy. At the peak of evil's plot against him, Jesus cried out, *"Father, forgive them, for they know not what they do!"*

This act demonstrated that no matter how entrenched we are in the discord of evil, there are open arms welcoming us back to our true family and origin!

Yes, Jesus's blood brings us back into the arms of the Trinity. There is no better place to explore this incredible mystery than in another passage from Hebrews 10. Pay particular attention to the final sentence, for this will lead us back to the Shulamite's story.

> *And now we are brothers and sisters in God's family because of the blood of Jesus, and he welcomes us to come into the most holy sanctuary in the heavenly realm—boldly and without hesitation. For he has dedicated a new, life-giving way for us to approach God. For just as the veil was torn in two, Jesus' body was torn open to give us free and fresh access to him!*
> –Hebrews 10:19-20 TPT

It is this "life-giving way" that the Shepherd King is leading his seeking Shulamite. He is taking her down the only road where we can experience lasting freedom from the veil that covers our lives and robs our DNA of its destiny. As such, it is the pathway that takes us to the unimaginable treasures that kicked off this entire journey.

Day Twelve:
Hidden Glory

By poetry, prophecy, and proverb, we find the scriptures comparing humanity's deepest problem to a prostitute wearing a dark veil. Thankfully, in the passage we just read, good news has invaded the scene. Jesus's death firmly dealt with this lying veil. In fact, at the moment of his passing, an actual "veil" inside the temple of Jerusalem was torn in half:

> *Then the sun was darkened, and the veil of the temple was torn in two. And when Jesus had cried out with a loud voice, He said, "Father, 'into Your hands I commit My spirit.'" Having said this, He breathed His last.*
> –Luke 23:45-46 NKJV

Right as Jesus was giving his last breath for the world, the veil that covered the innermost room of the temple—the most sacred site in all Israel—was cut right down the middle.

A little bit of history might be helpful here. The temple of Jerusalem was at the center of Israel's faith. It was designed after the original temple built by the same man who wrote the Song of Songs. Solomon—the one who linguistically "built" the Shulamite—is the same person who built the temple. Consequently, both the Shulamite and the temple represent the same thing: humanity.

Solomon's temple had three parts to it: the Outer Court, the Holy Place, and the Holy of Holies. This corresponds to human beings, who are described as having three main parts: body, soul, and spirit (1 Thessalonians 5:23). The body is the Outer Court of our being. Just as the Outer Court of the temple was exposed to outside elements, so are our bodies. This is what everyone sees when they look at us.

The Holy Place, however, was hidden. This speaks to the next layer of our being—the soul, the seat of our personality, emotions, and will. And yet deeper within the temple was the Holy of Holies, the place that housed the most important part of the entire structure: the Ark of the Covenant. The Ark was the very throne of God's presence—the place of his manifest glory.

This tiny unseen room corresponds to a person's spirit—the innermost part of their being that supplies life to their soul and body. This is the original breath of God, which we can also call his "image" and "glory." This resides in all people. In the book of Job, it says that all flesh would cease to exist if God were to withdraw "his breath and his Spirit" (Job 34:14-15).

Every human is a temple. We were made to be a vessel for the divine Spirit to flow like a river into our souls and then out through our physical bodies as a blessing of love, joy, and peace to the world around us.

Interestingly, within Solomon's temple was a thick veil set up to block the way to that innermost room. This veil prevented people from seeing and experiencing the glory of God at its center. A giant piece of fabric was set up to communicate the same message as the Shulamite's veil. They both speak to our spiritual prostitution and our efforts at earning union.

Some readers will know that Solomon's Temple was designed after an even older structure known as Moses's tabernacle. This tent also represented humanity as it wandered around the wilderness for forty years. The veiled, wandering tabernacle speaks to the same thing as the Shulamite. It is the life of going around in circles, ever trying to find the promise of true life yet constantly falling back into the dust of our failures.

All this is to say that a dark veil covers the image-bearing heart of the human race—a veil that has been calloused and hardened by the ancient deception: *I am dark. And my Creator is dark as well…* This is the original distortion of the music, where we lost sight of Love's true face—and our own face as well.

Over time, this veil became so thick no one could see through it—let alone tear it down. Systems of religion were created with rituals and processes aimed at reattaining what we knew to be true somewhere inside us. With this came exquisite philosophies communicating grand ideas about the true self. Spiritual gurus have talked about the light within and provided guidance on meditation and manipulations of the mind. However, nothing could overcome the power of this veil. To bring it down, we needed something greater than ourselves.

We needed help—or *saving*.

And hence came our Creator, arriving on earth in the form of a Jewish person called Yeshua—a Hebrew name meaning "God is Salvation." This Man, who many know through the English name Jesus, came to do what we could not do on our own—what religion and philosophy could not do either.

He came to tear down the veil.

And this is exactly what happened when he exhaled his last breath on the cross.

The Identity of God

Remember, Jesus is the One who gave us that first release of breath when we were formed from the dust. This was the kiss that birthed humanity into life—our original blessing. Now, at the cross, our Creator exhales once again. He releases breath in order to awaken us from the dust once more, only this time it is the dust of spiritual sleep.

This is what is going on in Hebrews 10, the passage we looked at in the last chapter. It says there that Jesus's body became "the veil." That's significant, considering there's another scripture that says Jesus "became sin" for us (2 Corinthians 5:21). This is because the "veil" and "sin" are one and the same. The word *sin* is not primarily about behavior, but rather a deception that grew into an overwhelming force of darkness in our lives (which certainly affected our behavior).

And this deception is simple: it is unbelief in the goodness of God.

But when Jesus came to earth, these lies were dismantled. His entire life was a song of truth—singing and declaring the true identity of God. This is why he would often say, "If you've seen me, you've seen the Father" (John 14:9).

One of the ways he revealed the Father was by constantly coming against the things that bring sorrow and loss into the world. He calmed violent storms, healed every sickness presented to him, and defeated death itself. He demonstrated that destruction and death do not come from God; rather, they emerge from lies and from the dark forces that father and nurture those lies (see John 8:44 and 10:10)

Through a life of melodious grace, this promised Savior completely nixed false ideas about God. But the song of his life reached its crescendo in his final moments. His last act of suffering forever proved that God is not wrathful in the sense of condemning punishment. As the Lamb of God, Jesus redefined these archaic and broken ideas about the anger of God. His wrath is not against us, but against anything that robs his children of life.

God came to earth with a ferocious lion-like love in order to rescue us. And he did this with such passion that even if we resisted him by murdering him along the way, he would still stretch out his arms and leave us with an eternal roar of forgiveness.

This is why he is called both the Lion and the Lamb.

The Meal on the Table

Humanity has fallen asleep, lost in a nightmare that has twisted the face of God, and we are now unable to wake ourselves up. But Jesus came as the kiss of God to wake us up from this spell. He came and lived a life of unwavering grace, which was poured out fully in the form of a crucified body.

This is what is set before us at the table of the Lamb. Through communion, we remember the truth of Christ—particularly his work on the cross. The cross is the only message that carries a sword sharp enough to cut through the thick fabric of our institutionalized deception. It is the only "music" that matches (and thus re-tunes us to) the original sound of creation.

Before we go deeper into Solomon's poetry, let's look at one more relevant scripture:

> *But to this day whenever Moses* (the religious law) *is read, a veil lies over their heart; but whenever a person turns to the Lord, the veil is taken away. Now the Lord is the Spirit, and where the Spirit of the Lord is, there is liberty. But we all, with unveiled face, beholding as in a mirror the glory of the Lord, are being transformed into the same image from glory to glory, just as from the Lord, the Spirit.*
> –2 Corinthians 3:15-18 (parenthesis mine)

At the table, we not only remember the truth of who God is as a good and rescuing Father, but we also see who we are, for it says we behold him *as in a mirror.* His face reveals the truth about ours.

And this makes sense when we recognize that Jesus, the Savior of the world, is both perfect God *and* perfect Man. In the next part of the poem, we'll see this even more…

Day Thirteen:
Sensory Experience

Revelation light is dawning. Our symbol-cracking shovels are striking the outer layer of the treasure box and we're now going to continue digging deeper into its mysteries.

We've found ourselves at a table. In response to the Shulamite's desire for rest, the Shepherd led her to the revelation of "Christ and him crucified" (1 Corinthians 2:2). Along with this message of Christ's redemption, a table is also a symbol of fellowship and belonging. It's important we see this as well.

Tables are where friends and family gather. When sitting around a table there is a sense of equality and shared life. There's little room to hide at a table. When you sit down, your face is visible to everyone there. Thankfully, food provides a divine buffer for the raw intimacy of conversation, helping us go deeper down the path of connection.

Now, you'll remember the Shulamite's "mother's sons"—the ones who brought grief and burnout into her life. These are the ones who put religion above the table of fellowship. This is why Jesus came not only to tear down the veil but to overthrow entire religious temples with their regulations and mantras. He came to break down every sweat-producing system that puts rules, performance, and money over the hearts of human beings.

And so, the invitation to a table is truly the answer to her heart's desires, and it is here that she encounters another powerful symbol. This will bring us back to the main meal on the menu—the divine pathway and buffer that will enable us to grow in that intimate connection we seek.

The Kiss of Christ

Tears of a Tree

A sachet of myrrh is my lover,
like a tied-up bundle of myrrh resting over my heart.
He is like a bouquet of henna blossoms—
henna plucked near the vines at the fountain of the Lamb.
I will hold him and never let him part.
–Song 1:13-14 TPT

The Shulamite begins to hold a "bundle of myrrh" over her heart. This ancient spice is symbolically associated with suffering, partly because of the resin that emerges like teardrops on the bark of its tree. In fact, the ancients called it "tears of a tree." During biblical times, it was also used for embalming bodies in preparation for burial.

The Shulamite holding myrrh over her heart is a clear visual of someone taking hold of the revelation of Jesus's suffering and receiving it into the depths of their being. She is smelling the ascending scent of love that flowed from his act of sacrificial grace. Though there is still much to learn, the Shulamite is starting to meditate upon the unimaginable... *The Creator of heaven and earth suffered and died for me.*

This is not some religious story she's thinking about. She is feeding on a tangible reality that has the power to water the growing desert in her soul. The message of the cross was never meant to be an old tale confined just to sermons, religious paintings, and jewelry. It was meant to be a sensory experience. We are called not just to know it in our heads but to take it in like fragrance from a spice rising into the nostrils and affecting all our senses.

On that note, she also takes in the smell of henna blossoms, which were known for their especially pleasing fragrance. These spices were found all over an area called En-Gedi, rightly rendered in the above translation as the "Fountain of the Lamb." In the same way that myrrh speaks of death, henna speaks of Jesus's resurrection. And of course, the two events go hand in hand.

The resurrection of Jesus was the supernatural confirmation of all the truths we've been digging into. Now the Shulamite is enjoying the fruit of what the cross accomplished. She is taking in the truth that she is of like value to the King of Glory!

Return of the Dove

If you're someone who has a hard time accepting this message (i.e., something is stuffing up your spiritual sinuses and keeping you from inhaling its truths), the next passage may help break up the clog.

As the Shulamite partakes of the meal on the table, inhaling and exhaling its smells, a new perspective begins to dawn. Her spiritual senses are awakened. She begins to "hear" the music of creation. Her eyes begin to "see," especially when the King calls her to *behold* what he himself sees:

How beautiful you are, my darling,

How beautiful you are!

Your eyes are like doves.

To which the Shulamite responds:

> *How handsome you are, my beloved...*
> –Song 1:15-16

Twice the King calls her "beautiful." With these words, God is cutting through the outer layer of her unbelief. He's breaking through the burnt-out shell of weariness and declaring the beauty inside. In other words, he's revealing what the cross has bought back ("redeemed").

Now, our English Bibles translate the King's words as "beautiful" or "lovely," while the Shulamite's returning compliment is rendered "handsome." But in the Hebrew, all these words are the same.

Think about that. This poetry is about us and God. God is calling her (us!) the same term for beauty that she uses for him. This speaks of our identity as image-bearers. We are beautiful, lovely, and delightful because we look just like the Beautiful One. (And this is said to her while the veil still lies over her face!)

Earlier, we saw Paul address this with the Cornthian church. He said that when we turn to the Lord, it's like looking in a mirror. Such is the case with Solomon and the Shulamite using the same term of beauty to describe one another.

And there's something else the King speaks over her. After calling her divinely beautiful, he makes an absolutely wild declaration: he tells her she has *dove's eyes*.

Do you remember the image of the dove hovering over Noah's floodwaters, or the dove landing on Christ in the Jordan River? This bird is a clear symbol of the Holy Spirit, the One who fluttered over the first waters of creation in Genesis 1. By comparing her eyes to doves, he is comparing us to *his very Spirit*. He is gazing past the false veil and exposing the glory that is still inside!

We're not stretching this interpretation by making the text say whatever we want. The dove is an obvious symbol sitting gently upon the metaphoric wrapping paper of the poem. Some may choose to stay on the outer "literal" layer and assert that this is some kind of cute nickname an infatuated king gives to his mistress. But we are digging far deeper than that realm of interpretation.

This is speaking to the restoration of our original blessing—the blessing spoken over Adam and Eve, repeated over Noah and his family, then fully unveiled through Jesus in the Jordan River … It is this life-giving truth:

You are my lovely, beautiful, delightful child in whom I am well-pleased!

We're starting to see that the Song of Solomon is essentially one big encounter with this harmonious revelation. This is the "kiss" the Shulamite was seeking from the beginning. The revelation of the cross, the truth of God's suffering love, the redemption of our true selves. This is the Song of all songs, and it is the same reality the book of Revelation calls the Song of the Lamb.

This Song is the reckoning that comes upon the hardness of human hearts, transforming the harlot wandering in the wilderness into who she really is…a rising Bride!

DAY FOURTEEN: NEW WINE

Immersed in the fragrance of redemption and all its fruits, the Shulamite sings out the following words in a new chorus of confidence:

I am the rose of Sharon...
—Song 2:1

In The Passion Translation, there's a note about the word *Sharon*. One way the original Hebrew for this term can be rendered is "his song." The verse is therefore put like this:

I am truly his rose,
The very theme of his song.

Do you see the wonder of this statement? Going all the way back to our expedition through the glass eyes of giant telescopes and the vibrational origins of creation, we remember how the universe is one song—and its growing chorus plays on the strings of our DNA. Creation's ultimate purpose is humanity. We are the "very theme" of the music God sang out in Genesis 1!

At the same time, the theme of creation is God himself—the One humanity reflects.

Yes, the beauty of the triune Family is whispered through the families of star systems and animal habitats, but it's shouted in the intimate relationships of human beings (when we walk in true love and servanthood). There, the infinite dimensions of God somehow unfold into time and space.

As she tastes redemption's kiss, the Shulamite is discovering the meaning of her existence. This revelation—of being the song of his heart and the theme of his music—brings her back to her earlier focus:

Like an apple tree among the trees of the woods,
So is my beloved among the sons.
I sat down in his shade with great delight,
And his fruit was sweet to my taste.
–Song 2:3

The table of the King has transformed into a new symbol. She now finds herself under the shade of a tree. Thankfully, cracking open the meaning of this symbol doesn't require much effort, since it holds the same essential meaning as the table. In fact, the meaning is even clearer because it was at a literal tree where Christ poured out redemption's blood. On a hill known as Calvary, Jesus Christ was crucified on wood from a cut-down tree.

The Shulamite is finding her rest under the reality of what Jesus did. As she comes to see perfect love hanging from a tree, the worth of her own soul is being restored. The severe burns of religion streaking across her soul—as well as the cuts from sin's thorns in which she's been entangled—all are finding healing. The shadow under which she sits releases a soothing balm of forgiveness and grace over these deep wounds.

We were made to sit under the shade of a smiling Father—a truly good God who stands in our defense and defines us by his love. When taken into the heart, this truth becomes a sweet-tasting fruit to the soul. It's like eating from the Tree of Life, the place we were originally meant to abide under and never leave.

Yes, we were made to know continually that we are the delight of heaven. The same desire we see in children for their parents' attention and affection is resonant in every heart, no matter how old we may get. The words *"you are my beloved child"* were meant to fill our hearts every day. We were made to know we have the Father's complete and perfect adoration.

The Shulamite is taking her fill of this heavenly food and, as a result, she's ushered into a whole new world…

The House of Wine

He has brought me to his banquet hall,
And his banner over me was love.
–Song 2:4

The Shulamite's delight in Jesus's death and resurrection becomes a feast of celebration. We've gone from a table to myrrh to a tree and now back to something similar to a table—yet far grander. Suddenly, the Shulamite finds herself transported into what most English translations call "the banquet hall." Yet this Hebrew phrase is better translated as *house of wine*.

Like the dove, we've found wine to be a clear symbol for the Holy Spirit. In the beginning of the Song, wine was compared to the Shepherd's love, which is quite fitting when we consider how scripture makes these two statements about God:

God is love…
–1 John 4:8

And in the same chapter:

…God is Spirit.
–John 4:24

In this poetic statement, the Shulamite is diving deep into the love of God—which is to say she is drinking in the very Spirit of God. And this isn't just a little sip. This is now a whole house stocked with barrels upon barrels of sweet, intoxicating love. And like natural wine, it's a love that changes your disposition as well as your confidence levels.

We've also seen how the Spirit of God is the kiss who brought that original blessing of life to humanity. This is what the Shulamite sought in the beginning when she longed to be free from her striving. Now she has found not just one small kiss of grace but an overabundant banquet of love and affirmation.

The "house of wine" represents a rich and full experience of God's loving Spirit. However, it's important to see how this experience comes *after* she learns to sit under the finished work of Christ. This is the key note and secret chord of the entire Song.

Yes, everything comes down to feasting upon what God has provided through Jesus. This is what the prophet Isaiah writes about when he reminds his listeners that the "wine" of God is not something you purchase or earn:

> *Ho! Every one who thirsts, come to the waters;*
> *And you who have no money come, buy and eat.*
> *Come, buy wine and milk*
> ***Without money and without cost.***
> –Isaiah 55:1 (emphasis mine)

The wine is a gift. Our only requirement is trust.

Yes, as we run back into the arms of our Creator, joyfully accepting what we've tasted at the banquet table, a liberty within our souls comes forth. Springs of life that were once locked away come rushing out of our innermost being. The ancient veil on our hearts finally splits open, revealing the true Holy of Holies within. Unleashed is the precious gift of our original blessing, emerging like water as it sings its way over the dry riverbed of our lives.

And this leads us to the most stunning conclusion…

We *are* the house of wine!

Our bodies are temples of intoxicating grace. And as the veil is cut by the sword of Christ's cross, the flow of this grace is effortless and free.

With all of this in her purview, the Shulamite speaks the next phrase with stunning clarity:

His banner over me is love!

The Creator God has planted a flag of victory over her entire life. Whether it's her past, present, or future—the Shulamite is surrounded and defined by this immense and eternal love of her Divine Family. This is the theme and glory of her life. It's why she's here—and it's where's she headed.

The awakening has begun. The Shulamite sees the banner that defines everything else. Unfortunately, as so often happens, something will try to creep back in and sew up these new openings in her veil. Before we get there, though, let's step back and take in another *selah*.

Selah

Let's take another decisive pause.

Hidden within the poetry of scripture is a little line that goes like this:

There is a river whose streams make glad the city of God, the holy dwelling places of the Most High.
–Psalm 46:4–

If each of us is a house for God, then all of us together form a city. Jesus affirmed this when he called his disciples a city on a hill. According to this Psalm, there is a river of life sparkling with delight and running through this city…*through us*. And this river makes every individual "house" glad.

Joy, delight, and relaxation are part of our inheritance. But these are not feelings we conjure up or force. They are the result of a tangible movement of Life coursing through our being.

This river will assuredly flow when we allow the love of God and the truths surrounding the cross to fill our hearts. Like the Shulamite bringing a bundle of myrrh to her chest, we are called to let the aroma of grace penetrate the chambers of our skull and break the veils that bind up our joy.

Let us take a moment—or two or three—and close our eyes to see Jesus hanging from a tree. Gaze into his eyes of compassion as he looks down upon you, blood dripping from his brow and yet a heart overflowing with love—passionate and transforming.

He looks at you and calls you *his delightful one.*

You are beautiful, lovely, and good.

Very good.

Perfect.

Movement Three

Asleep

Day Fifteen:
A Lingering Spell

Rising from the ashes of discord, the Song of the Lamb breaks forth through the mouth of the Shulamite. As she experiences the great banner of her Creator's love, the Song reaches a climax.

But the story is far from over. There are things that stand opposed to this holy crescendo. Before she can come into full harmony with creation's original song, something tries to pull her back down into the dust. And this is how it goes sometimes: the journey of grace can seem like two steps forward and one back (and that one step back can feel more like thirteen).

Look carefully at her next words:

> *Sustain me with raisin cakes,*
> *Refresh me with apples,*
> *Because I am lovesick.*
> *Let his left hand be under my head*
> *And his right hand embrace me.*
> –Song 2:5-6

It may be hard to see at first, but something begins to change here. Up to this point, the Shulamite has taken her seat at the table of grace and eaten from the truths of redemption. She has inhaled the sweet revelation that she is the very theme of his song. She's a temple of his glory, bearing his beauty and likeness. She has encountered the One who says, *"I will never leave you nor will I ever forsake you."*

Nonetheless, she suddenly confesses a sense of separation. The Shulamite uses the word *lovesick* to describe herself. This is one of two times this word appears (see Song 5:8). It signifies her desire to be back in the King's presence—as though something is in the way of their union.

The word for "sick" in *lovesick* is the Hebrew term for disease and brokenness. It was also used for grief because it applied to all types of loss and pain experienced throughout the world. Such grief is what led her into spiritual harlotry in the first place when she perceived a lack in the love department. This drove her to search for love in all kinds of unhealthy ways—such as religiosity, addiction, or broken relationships.

According to the prophet Isaiah, this is exactly what Jesus took on our behalf at the cross. The same word for *sick* is used in Isaiah 53, where we find a vivid depiction of Jesus's taking away our "grief" and "sickness" through his suffering. This gives even more context as to why Jesus brought her to the table of communion before anything else.

The cross was—and is—the answer for this pain in her heart. It was there she sat under the tree and experienced all the love she was looking for. It was there she tasted the truth that she's been given an unbreakable union with God.

But in this part of the Song, the Shulamite loses sight of this union once more. Like Eve in the garden, something brings her into the feeling of being dark—and of God being distant from her. Perhaps she started to see something in her life, a certain habit or attitude, that made her feel she was no longer pleasing to her Maker. Maybe she assumed God was losing patience with her in the maturing process. Perhaps she encountered some kind of painful circumstance that made her doubt God's love for her.

Whatever it is, there are countless reasons why people lose sight of their union with God and "fall asleep" to his loving presence. Such spiritual sleep is common when we encounter God's love but then go on to *feel* or *see* something contradictory in our lives. We hear the song of grace resonating in the depths of our being, but if we're not careful, false notes of guilt and fear can seep in and lull us back to sleep.

In this passage, we see the Shulamite making a request to the King: *"Let his left hand be under my head, and his right hand embrace me."* The left hand under the head and the right hand embracing her is a picture of physical intimacy. As we've shown, this is pointing to the higher reality of union with God. Therefore, this is a prayer for union and connection.

It makes sense that she would make this request since we've just seen her confess her lovesickness (and we'll see her sense of separation from God in other ways as the chapter goes on). This might seem like a noble request, but it becomes a problem when it arises from a deceived place—where someone is grieving something that is not truly lost.

Spiritual Bewitchment

There is a letter in the New Testament written to a group of awakened "Shulamites" who had also begun to fall back asleep just like the heroine of Solomon's ballad. The apostle Paul writes to these people—known as the Galatians—explaining how they have been bewitched, that a spell has been cast over their eyes:

> *What has happened to you foolish Galatians? Who has put you under an evil spell? Did God not **open your eyes** to see the meaning of Jesus' crucifixion? Was he not revealed to you as the crucified one?*
> –Galatians 3:1 TPT (emphasis mine)

Because of some form of their own lovesickness, the Galatian believers started looking for ways to become more connected with God and were going back under the veil of religion to reattain this connection. Like the Shulamite, they had forgotten the beautiful truths restored at the cross. Paul therefore reminds them that the old, sick, grieving identity is forever crucified with Jesus. They are new creations now, completely one with their Creator (Galatians 6:14-16).

The fact that the Shulamite is spiritually asleep is revealed even further by the King's response. This is where we see Jesus speaking to a group of people called "the daughters of Jerusalem," who are watching this whole poem play out. As onlookers of the Shulamite's journey, they represent all of us who are called to learn from her experience and discover our own unveiling:

I adjure you, O daughters of Jerusalem,
By the gazelles or by the hinds of the field,
That you do not arouse or awaken my love
Until she pleases.
–Song 2:7

As we've noted before, translation is very important. When the King speaks of "love," some versions miss the fact that he's referring to *his love*—that is, his beloved Shulamite. He is saying that *she* is the one sleeping. But instead of forcing her to wake up through fear and pressure, he wants us to know that awakening comes through the sweet song of grace. His love is not to be awakened until *she pleases*.

The word *pleases* comes from a Hebrew term that means delight and pleasure. This detail reinforces the fact that the religion of our "mother's sons"—the systems we've grown up in—cannot bring genuine awakening. That only happens when we taste God's goodness and trust the love poured out in Jesus's death and resurrection.

Thankfully, the King will continue to release his kiss of grace over her life. Though she will remain upon a bed of slumber for some time—her eyes opening and closing behind a sleepy veil—this prayer for the fruits of the cross to satisfy her soul will eventually be fulfilled.

The Historical Lie

A quick note to say that the journey of the Shulamite is the story of Christianity as a whole. The Song of Songs is the story of an individual believer learning to awake and arise, and it is also the story of the global church throughout history—for there is only one bride in the eyes of the King.

With the coming of Christ, the revelation of the ages dawned upon the world, sparking a revolution that not only split the temple veil in two but also the calendar of recorded history. Sadly, it was not long after this awakening that things began to shift. The "mother's sons" arose and brought chains of legalism into the church. As time went on, there were many other awakenings and reformations, but these were often followed by people quenching the Spirit's kiss with manmade systems and performance-based teachings.

Thankfully, the Song is far from over. As it goes on, we will see how relentless the Lord is in his pursuit of his on-and-off-again bride. There will be an awakening in her just as there will be an awakening in you—and in the entire world around you.

Let us keep moving forward then, for we've only just begun to strike the gold hidden in this poetry.

Day Sixteen: A Fractured Wall

Her eyes began to open, but the sleep of separation has now come back over the Shulamite's wandering heart. She finds herself in a kind of dream state, with the Shepherd's words echoing from some seemingly distant space. Beyond the shadows of her lost and barren feelings, the Shulamite acknowledges his voice as it grows in volume and intention:

> *The voice of my beloved!*
> *Behold, he comes*
> *Leaping upon the mountains,*
> *Skipping upon the hills.*
> *My beloved is like a gazelle or a young stag.*
> *Behold, he stands behind our wall;*
> *He is looking through the windows,*
> *Gazing through the lattice.*
> –Song 2:8-9 NKJV

Instead of a veil, we now see a "wall" between the Shulamite and her King. It's behind this wall that he stands, just as he stood behind the veil, and he calls to her with the same voice of truth. The text shows him peering into the windows of the wall, suggesting he is perhaps still looking into her eyes, which are like windows to the soul.

But these "windows" are partially closed because of a certain material covering them. To see into her, the King must gaze through *lattice*. This has an interesting connection to the veil and further explains what it means to be spiritually asleep.

Common on many ancient windows, lattice is a crisscrossed pattern of strips of building material, typically wood or metal. The design creates a weave or grid, allowing only a partial, broken-up view of what's outside—or inside—when one looks through it.

This serves as a striking metaphor for the Shulamite and her exodus out of spiritual harlotry. With latticework over her eyes, there is a degree of light coming through. However, depending on how tightly crisscrossed the lattice is, that light becomes scattered and divided.

Such imagery speaks to the journey of humanity, who has long looked out at God and the world through incomplete light. Mankind has looked and seen a fractured image of the Creator. As a result, his face is distorted—especially when it mixes with the "wood" of our own broken characteristics. In this fragmented view of God's face, our own face—our identity—also becomes broken. This leads to further lovesickness and enhances our sense of guilt and striving.

Religion's Dividing Nature

The apostle Paul tells us that Jesus came to tear down not only a veil, but also a dividing wall (Ephesians 2:14-15). They are, in fact, one and the same. This is what we now see in the Shulamite's story. She stands behind this ancient wall, which Paul connects to the law of Moses. The law, he says, divides us not only from God but also from one another.

In the Old Testament, the law was given through Moses to the people of Israel. Initially, this seemed to be a good thing. It taught how we should properly relate to God and to each other. Summarized in Ten Commandments, it told us to avoid lying, cheating, stealing, worshiping idols, and other destructive actions. These commands were then backed up by serious threats of punishment should anyone disobey.

Unfortunately, when we look back at the history of God's people, we find a long string of failures. The entire Old Testament shows a losing battle, as generation after generation struggles to live up to the standards of the law. By the time we reach the New Testament, we learn the reason: the law was never meant to be the true solution to our problem. Laws can guide and protect us, but what we truly need is a transformation of the heart and mind. We need to do the right thing not because of threats, but because it flows from who we are.

And this is exactly why Jesus came—to transform our hearts and restore our true identity as image-bearers. As image-bearers, we're designed to live in love. According to the letter to the Galatians, there's no need for a law when love is flourishing (Galatians 5:22-23).

One problem with the law was that people began trusting in their own ability to follow it. This meant they were trusting in themselves to secure God's favor and presence. In this way, it connects to the prostitute's veil, for it exposes our efforts to buy our way into union with God.

In reality, the law exposed our pride. What was meant to teach us love ended up doing the opposite. Our insecurities twisted it into a fuel source for jealousy, performance, and elitism. This is why it became a wall between people groups. The Jewish people began to believe their system of holy standards made them superior to the world around them.

But of course, this was not just a Jewish problem—it's a human one. The law of Moses simply exposed what all our systems tend to do. Noble and good as an outward law might appear, it does not deal with the root lies—that original distortion of the music.

The real problem is our blindness. We are veiled and walled behind a darkened view of God and self. Because of this, we also see others through a distorted lens. This leads us to feel unsafe and resistant to relationship and interdependence. In response, we build even higher walls of protection and create stronger systems of blame and punishment in hopes of keeping ourselves safe and everyone else in line. But in the end, this only serves to bolster our pride. As we fail to see ourselves as God's beloved children, we lose sight of others as members of the same treasured family.

And this is precisely why Jesus is *our peace*. He came to break down this latticework—this fractured view of God, self, and others. This dividing wall is what the Voice of the Beloved speaks through in the Song of Songs as he continues pouring out his kisses of truth on the Shulamite's sleeping heart.

Jesus looks at her and still sees her true face. Even though she hides behind a wall, he knows her destiny. He knows that she is custom-made for love—love for God, love for herself, and love for the world around her. For this reason, the following comes out of his mouth:

> *My beloved spoke, and said to me:*
> *"Rise up, my love, my fair one,*
> *And come away."*
> –Song 2:10 NKJV

Let's be very clear about something here. There are many teachings out there regarding this famous call to "come away." Many carry a harsh tone, as though Jesus is commanding her to enter a life of religious sacrifice and pain. Now, pain and sacrifice certainly come with the territory of following Jesus, but they are not our pursuit. (They find us quite easily on their own.) The call to "come away" is about leaving the dividing wall of religion! It's about leaving behind the false grief of separation from God and learning to trust in our union with the Divine Family.

This is the invitation. We are called to rise from our bed of bewitchment where a false sense of lack convinces us that Jesus is gone—and our lovesick souls must now strive to get him back.

It's also about waking up from the dream state of this world, where we view others through a lattice of blame and judgment.

Much of the Shulamite's path will involve embracing the world around her, for her destiny is to awaken others to this magnificent song of grace. But first, she must deal with this dividing wall. She must accept that the wall between her and others has been demolished by the blood of Jesus—the One called the *Son of Man*. He is the One who reveals that all mankind carries holy blood, worthy of his—and our—pursuit.

The Voice comes to her, and with that same secret chord we discovered earlier, she's invited to embrace its sound even more. And this chord is not just for her—it's also for the fractured and latticed people all around her. To them, the Lord sings the same message:

You are my delightful, pleasing children!

*You **all** make me feel real good inside.*

Day Seventeen:
The Awake Tree

Not long after the experience in Asia I mentioned earlier, I found myself in the nation of Israel having a powerful moment involving almond trees.

The moment was powerful primarily because of the timing and location. It was October 2017, and we had just announced a name change for our church community. After a clear prompting from the Lord, we changed the name to The Almond Branch. A week or so after this, I found myself unexpectedly seeing real almond trees for the first time—in Israel.

But God's hand was especially evident when I realized *where* I was in the country.

I saw these trees in the place Jesus himself grew up. The One whom the prophets called the "Branch" grew up in the town of Nazareth, which I learned most likely derived its name from a Hebrew term for branch—*netzer*.

Now, the Hebrew word *almond* literally means "to watch"—as with open eyes—or "to be awake." Thus, the almond tree has long been known in Hebrew tradition as the *Awake Tree*. It holds this title because it is the first tree to blossom in the winter. As early as late January, almond blossoms emerge like bright signal fires calling to the other trees and announcing that the time has come to awaken from winter's slumber.

This is the same call that comes to the Shulamite in her moment of unbelief. This voice of truth is radiating through the lattice over her wall, and it resounds with the following words:

The Kiss of Christ

The season has changed,
the bondage of your barren winter has ended,
and the season of hiding is over and gone.
The rains have soaked the earth
and left it bright with blossoming flowers.
The season for singing and pruning the vines has arrived.
I hear the cooing of doves in our land,
filling the air with songs to awaken you and guide you forth.
—Song 2:11-12 TPT

An Astounding Miracle

Let's pause and imagine something for a moment. Let's say there was a sheltered boy raised in a region high up in the north of a country like Greenland which, despite its name, does not know the green wonders of the earth. All this child has ever known are igloos, tundra, and snow. Imagine then that this young person has never accessed the internet and was never told about other climates. His only frame of reference for the outdoors is the strong and icy grip of winter.

Let's say you come to this young boy with two large photographs. The first is of a scene farther south, down in the northeastern United States during the dead of January. It is a giant field of snow surrounded by dead trees, their branches thick with ice and barely visible against the gray sky. The child would look at this and obviously see something very similar to the world he already knows.

But then you take out the second picture and tell him this is the same exact field. However, this picture was taken just a few months later. In the photo, an unbelievable transfiguration has taken place. An alien landscape of color now fills the scene. The mighty weight of snow is gone, replaced with majestic flowers and a sprawl of flying creatures encircling the trees that now bear multiple shades of green.

The Awake Tree

Imagine the sheer awe that would overtake such a child—this, mixed with a demanding curiosity questioning whether the image was real. And we couldn't blame him for such doubt. It's only because we experience seasonal changes that our brains dial down the wonder and impossibility of it all. The transformation of spring is an astounding miracle.

There is a very real way we can relate to this imaginary boy from Greenland. The reality is, we live in a world that is spiritually frozen, and the idea of a heavenly springtime on earth seems utterly preposterous. But in our state of original blessing, humanity was made to burst forth into a landscape of vibrant unity, flourishing joy, and supernatural peace.

Unfortunately, in this frozen era of sin, most have forgotten this truth and disbelieve its potential. While there may be patches of "green" here and there—fleeting moments of beauty and joy—a global terrain of awakened love seems like an AI-generated piece of fake news. But this is the reality the King announces to the Shulamite. The human soul is filled with glory, and it is destined to blossom with the full fruits of God's image.

As one who represents the soul still learning to wake up, the Shulamite has a hard time accepting all of this. Even though she's encountered bursts of clarifying sunlight here and there, we still find a lingering cold in her life. Somehow, she's still undergoing wintry experiences—whether it's personal mistakes, the failures of others, or painful circumstances that seem to contradict God's promises. Such things call her back to her bed, keeping her stuck behind the wall of doubt and fear. And thus, much like our boy from Greenland, the idea of a totally different reality seems ludicrous.

But ludicrous it is not. For divine seed lies underneath the thick snow of our unbelief. As crazy as it sounds, a springtime of glory is poised to break through the soil of even the hardest human hearts, including those badly frozen behind walls of grief, skepticism, and religiosity.

This is the message the King brings to the Shulamite. In fact, he tells her that this glorious springtime has *already come*.

How the Ice Melts

In case you've forgotten, the King in this story is Jesus Christ. Earlier in the Song we looked at the glory of his crucifixion and all that this event communicates. Now we come to the power of his resurrection, the world-changing moment that followed his tragic death.

Jesus emerged from a tomb, one not unlike the countless graves covering the earth like pale frost, binding bodies into a frozen void. His resurrection was the "first-fruits" of a new spring. As the One who stands in our place—representing humanity's true and full identity—the resurrection of Christ reveals that beneath the weight of our darkness lies a seed of indestructible glory.

Jesus was and is the true almond tree. For this reason, he calls to the Shulamite—to the human soul still feeling the frozen pressures of life. He calls through the guilt, shame, and unbelief still bringing sleep to her eyes and covering her in a spiritual tomb. His words crack through the walls as he tells her that resurrection glory is here, no matter what her outward experiences may be. Indeed, it's already inside, waiting to break forth.

Such a message is possible because we are truly in union with Jesus. We were united with him in his death as well as in the momentous occasion of his resurrection. This is a key part of the "kiss" our sleeping souls need to receive. We are one with the risen Christ—and thus we can begin accessing this eternal springtime now.

The Awake Tree

...We have been co-resurrected with him so that we could be empowered to walk in the freshness of new life. For since we are permanently grafted into him to experience a death like his, then we are permanently grafted into him to experience a resurrection like his and the new life that it imparts.
—Romans 6:4-5 TPT

Even though it may feel impossibly hidden, the life and joy of the Spirit are ready to bud upon the branches of our lives. We can arise like Christ, for each of us is a branch on the eternal almond tree of his glory.

Buried beneath the darkness, this promise of humanity remains. And this is a promise for the entire cosmos. Our fine-tuned universe is destined to bloom with the colors of a triune spring. The resurrected Christ is the glad announcement of this. He is the first-fruits of it, and we are called to join him in a harvest of divine life.

On that note, there's a holiday the Hebrew people were given during the celebration of the first-fruits of the spring harvest. Many know it by the name Pentecost. In the book of Acts, the Spirit of God came during this special feast; however, instead of a dove, the Spirit appeared as flames of fire.

Fire, of course, is what melts ice. In the same way, the gift of God's Spirit breaks down our icy barrenness and releases a garden within. The Shulamite began to taste of this earlier but unfortunately cowered back behind her wall. Nonetheless, the Lord comes to her again, encouraging her by saying, *"I hear the cooing of doves in our land."* He's reminding her that Pentecost has come. We are not waiting for something new. We are waking up to what has already been released in the resurrection of Jesus.

And with that, his words continue:

*Can you not discern this new day of destiny breaking forth
around you?
The early signs of my purposes and plans are bursting forth.
The budding vines of new life are now blooming everywhere.
The fragrance of their flowers whispers,
"There is change in the air."
Arise, my love, my beautiful companion,
and run with me to the higher place.
For now is the time to arise and come away with me.*
–Song 2:13 TPT

The call is clear. The time has come to step into the fullness of her identity and calling.

Unfortunately, in this next part, we'll see how the core lie of separation from God continues to cloud her perspective and dampen the sound of his voice…

Day Eighteen:
Fox and Dove

The Shulamite's journey heralds the voice of the Maker to every human soul: *The new day has come! Wake up from your slumber!*

Through her story, we also see how the soul resists such words. Thankfully, the King does not abandon his pursuit of us. His words of grace continue to flow like a river of irresistible force:

> *For you are my dove, hidden in the split-open rock.*
> *It was I who took you and hid you up high*
> *in the secret stairway of the sky.*
> *Let me see your radiant face*
> *and hear your sweet voice...*
> −Song 2:14 TPT

We have some new symbols to crack open here—particularly the "split-open rock." When we unfold the larger treasure map of scripture, the meaning of this is unmistakable. This is a reference to another part of the Old Testament when the children of Israel wandered through the desert. At one point, they approached their leader with a frantic demand to quench their growing thirst, prompting God to tell Moses to speak to a nearby rock. God promised that if he did this, water would miraculously burst forth from it.

Unfortunately, Moses didn't listen. Instead of speaking to the rock, he struck it with his rod multiple times. But by the grace of God, water still gushed out, and the people's thirst was quenched (Numbers 20:11).

In the New Testament, this strange story is unveiled as a prophetic image of Jesus, the One who is called the "Rock" (1 Corinthians 10:4). Jesus is the Rock who would be struck by religious leaders who literally used Moses's laws against him. Yet God would still pour out grace through this terrible act.

Though Jesus's body was pierced—*split open*—by the religious system of his day, water flowed from his side, and a torrent of healing was released to humanity (John 19:34). Jesus is now the "split-open rock" from which we drink. Now, in Solomon's poem, the King refers to the Shulamite as a dove hidden within this pierced rock.

Deep Calls to Deep

If you remember, at the beginning of her journey, the Shulamite came to the Shepherd with a deep thirst, much like the Israelites in the desert. He has been answering this request all along by giving her the kiss of truth. We discovered that the only thing that can water the garden of our souls and bring forth a springtime of resurrection glory is the kiss of his loving word—the reality of our original blessing.

Sadly, because of the lattice over her heart, it's been difficult for the Shulamite to receive. But by comparing her once more to a dove, the Shepherd continues to speak the word of original blessing into her weary heart. He is still answering her request.

And now, he goes deeper—calling her a dove *hidden within his wounds*.

This poetic picture of Jesus's work on the cross depicts us as the beloved of God, surrounded and covered by grace. Anything that speaks contrarily to our "dove" identity has been separated from us. In other words, the sin that stood opposed to us and condemned us has been crucified with Christ's body. He took away the judgment of the law, bearing it in his own body when he was struck down at Calvary. Because of this, we are no longer defined by the accusations that wage war against our souls.

As this kiss of good news penetrates the Shulamite's walls, we come to this other aspect of its message. For the King goes on to tell her she is hidden in *"the secret stairway of the sky."* He's calling her to wake up and smell the full truth of her union with Jesus. Not only are her sins taken care of through his crucifixion; she is also co-resurrected with him.

So, when the King says, *"Let me see your radiant face and hear your sweet voice,"* he is inviting her to come away from the wall that doubts this reality.

In the next verses, we'll see some of the underlying cement holding her wall together. This will provide more understanding as to why it's still a factor in her relationship with God.

Our Core Problem

Catch the foxes for us,
The little foxes that are ruining the vineyards,
While our vineyards are in blossom.
–Song 2:15

The Shulamite speaks of the sly little creatures that sneak through the fencing around vineyards and eat away at newly budding grapes. Grapes, of course, are the main ingredient in wine—another recurring symbol packed with treasure. It appears the Shulamite understands that the "vineyard" of the Spirit's life is blossoming within her. Yet behind her sleepy wall of fear, she worries about things eating away at this life—things that steal love, joy, peace, and every other variety of his heavenly vintage (Galatians 5:22-23).

Now, this seems like another noble request, but in the final part of her statement, we see how a deep lie is still influencing her perspective. Look closely at her next words:

My beloved is mine, and I am his.
He feeds his flock among the lilies.
Until the day breaks
And the shadows flee away,
Turn, my beloved,
And be like a gazelle
Or a young stag
Upon the mountains of Bether.
–Song 2:16-17 NKJV

To spot this lie, we must do some more digging into the original language of the poem. This passage begins with a beautiful declaration that the Shulamite belongs to her Beloved. This is wonderful. It shows just how far she has come. Even in her weakness, the Song of the Lamb is breaking through. The victorious banner of love is beginning to roll off her tongue with greater ease.

And yet a sour note creeps through. Like a little fox, discord enters the Song as the Shulamite rejects his invitation and tells him to turn away. Though she acknowledges their love, she says she will not come away from her wall *"until the day breaks and the shadows flee away."*

The reason, we find, is that she's waiting for the darkness around her—and whatever she perceives within herself—to completely vanish ("flee away"). Until this happens, she believes she cannot receive the word that calls her a precious dove. In other words, because of some lingering darkness, the Shulamite cannot *come away* from the wall that fragments her views of God and of herself.

This is not far from the attitude that rejects God's entire existence due to the bad things happening in the world. Though the Shulamite is not denying the reality of God, neither is she embracing the fullness of what he says about her. This is due to shadows—dark things she sees playing out in her life, whether by her own choices or the choices of those around her.

There's also a hint here that she is waiting for what the scriptures call "the day of the Lord"—what many understand to be the time of Christ's physical return to earth. Because of this, the Shulamite has a hard time accepting that a springtime of resurrection glory has already come, and that she is already lovely, perfect, and victorious.

In light of all this, it seems she does not want to walk by faith in her Beloved's kiss...

This insinuation is confirmed by her final statement, where she compares her Beloved to a gazelle running on a specific mountain range in Israel called Bether. This is yet another symbolic term unveiling a mystery to the seeking reader. In Hebrew, the name *Bether* means "division" or "separation." This tells us the Shulamite sees Christ in all his resurrected glory as *separate* from her.

One day, she says, *the shadows will flee away. Then Jesus will return, and all the promises of the end of the age will manifest. Then our faith will be made sight, and we can join our King on the mountain of victorious living. But for now, there are shadows and foxes getting in the way.*

But this is not the Shepherd's perspective. Instead, he invites her to rise like an almond tree blossoming with resurrection life, even while the unbelieving world still experiences a lingering "winter."

This part of the poem captures so poignantly the fractured beliefs of Christians throughout the ages. We confess that our

Beloved is fully ours—we are in him and he in us—yet we still live and sing and pray as though union is far away. We feel it can only be attained by scaling massive walls of religious sacrifice and effort. Deep down, however, we believe this union isn't attainable until we die and go to heaven—or until *the day breaks* and Jesus returns.

But what if this is the real fox? What if the little lie slipping in is the denial of our perfect union with our Beloved *right now*?

Yes, a global springtime of resurrection will manifest across the nations in ways beyond our imagination. There is great hope for the future. But why should we limit ourselves today? Why give in to the lie that says the blossoming of our true identity is not ours yet—and that his beauty and fragrance do not dwell upon us at this very moment?

Oh, maybe partially, we say. *But we can't claim it all for ourselves just yet. The dove that landed on Jesus remained there, but it only sits on our shoulders momentarily—and only if we're reading our Bible, fasting, or praying intensely. Most of the time, however, the dove just leaves and hovers, waiting for us to fight off more shadows.*

But this is the crux of the matter. Shadows do not have any substance! That sense of a lingering separation from God is a dark nothingness. Therefore, the call remains the same:

Arise, my love, into the truth
that you are already one with me
in both my death and resurrection.

Yes, you are my perfect dove,
hidden in the eternal shelter of my wounds,
and raised into the heights of heaven's wonders!

DAY NINETEEN: BABYLON AND ZION

Earlier, we took a wide-angle shot of the treasure map of the written word. We saw a panoramic view of the human journey captured in two opposing images—a veiled harlot and an unveiled bride. In parallel to these feminine metaphors is the same truth expressed architecturally. Across scripture, right to the very end, we find two opposing cities: the city of Babylon and the city of Zion—or, as it's called in the book of Revelation, the "New Jerusalem."

Metaphors only go so far, so utilizing a city instead of a woman reveals different facets of the same truth. In this case, the city imagery speaks to the human race as a whole, including our transfer from an economy of darkness into the prosperity of God's original image.

This metaphor appears in this next part of the Song, as we see the veiled Shulamite going on a fruitless search through a city:

On my bed night after night I sought him
Whom my soul loves;
I sought him but did not find him.
I must arise now and go about the city;
In the streets and in the squares
I must seek him whom my soul loves.
I sought him but did not find him.
 –Song 3:1-2

Before this scene, the Shulamite was behind her wall, resisting the Shepherd's call to come away. Now we see her lying in a bed, which we can only assume is where she has been the whole time. The veil, the wall, and now a bed of sleep—all communicate the same message. It's the same as the veiled prostitute, which now connects to this city known as the Harlot Babylon (Revelation 17).

This all speaks to a world spiritually asleep to the grace and truth of God. It's the life of restlessness that builds entire governments and economies on the broken foundation of insecurity and striving.

The Shulamite starts seeking the Beloved while on her bed and finds nothing (which you'd expect if your search is limited to your bedframe). Such is the fruit of being spiritually asleep to our union with God. We end up striving after his presence in vain since there's a veil (or wall) keeping us from seeing the truth.

She then states her desire to rise and go about a city. This seems like a good thing at first, as though she's finally realizing she must leave her state of sleep. Unfortunately, he's not found in the city either. This is because the city is nothing more than a continued dream state, as she remains behind the false security of her wall. (We'll see how subsequent chapters reveal that she is still in bed dreaming.)

Going into the "streets" and "squares" of the city refers to entering the realm of religion to find God. This is the way of Babylon—the city of man's self-inspired and self-defined efforts at godliness.

The word *squares* is particularly telling. It literally means "a broad way." Jesus warned about the broad paths, saying that broad is the way leading to destruction, and narrow is the path to life (Matthew 7:13). The broad places are man's efforts—the splintered paths billions take throughout the world in a desperate search for true life. The narrow path, meanwhile, is so narrow that only one Man could fit through it. Christ and his finished work *is* the narrow path of salvation.

Now, keep in mind that at this point in her journey the Shulamite has already tasted Jesus's goodness. This scene does not necessarily mean she is searching for God through paths other than Christ. There are plenty of religious paths right within the world of Christendom. Such is the reason Paul wrote to a group of believers who had tasted grace and yet still needed the following reminder:

> *For you were included in the death of Christ and have died with him to the religious system and powers of this world. Don't retreat back to being bullied by the standards and opinions of religion...*
> –Colossians 2:20 TPT

It's interesting that before her venture down these different avenues, the Shulamite first says she must rise to go about the city. There is indeed a type of "rising" that looks like spiritual growth when it's actually what many call *self-righteousness*. It is a treadmill of self-effort that makes you feel like you're getting somewhere (if you put enough sweat into it), and yet it leads only to disappointment as you engage in repetitive cycles of guilt followed by renewed motivation followed by more guilt.

Paul addresses this when he continues his thoughts to the Colossians:

> *I know that these regulations look wise with their self-inspired efforts at worship, their policy of self-humbling, and their studied neglect of the body. But in actual practice they do honour, not to God, but to man's own pride.*
> –Colossians 2:22-23 PHILLIPS

The Kiss of Christ

The Fringes

Fortunately, the Shulamite's search brings her to the outer edges of the city. She comes across the watchmen—men who were posted at the walls surrounding ancient communities:

> *The watchmen who go about the city found me;*
> *I said, "Have you seen the one I love?"*
> *Scarcely had I passed by them,*
> *When I found the one I love.*
> *I held him and would not let him go,*
> *Until I had brought him to the house of my mother,*
> *And into the chamber of her who conceived me.*
> –Song 3:3-4 NKJV

Because she finally "passed by" these men, we can assume she is leaving the boundaries of the city. In other words, she's moving past the gatekeepers of systems built around guilt, shame, and dualistic identities. It should not be surprising, then, that she begins sensing her Beloved's presence once more.

Such is the path for many who find God in the outer fringes of man's systems—including well-intentioned "Christian" ones. So many, in their pursuit of something authentic, find themselves in the same place, moving to the edges of what others deem acceptable or normal.

The Shulamite has reencountered the Lover of her soul. Though we'll find she is still asleep and that more revelation is needed, this is a wonderful moment of relief. She continues to grow in her awareness of the Trinity's loving presence, even in the midst of perceived darkness.

In this moment of encouragement, something is stated that we'll return to much later—something holding a great mystery spanning all of scripture and all human history. In this fresh experience of God's presence, the Shulamite says she wants to bring her Shepherd into "the house of her mother." Without saying too much now, this speaks to something that arises naturally when we experience freedom. We long to share that freedom with others, especially those still bound up in religion. This is a desire in the Shulamite's heart that will grow and mature throughout the rest of her journey.

To be truly fruitful, however, she must first awaken more herself. Sadly, in the next verse, we see her in a continued state of sleep as the King repeats these words about his beloved one:

I adjure you, O daughters of Jerusalem,
By the gazelles or by the hinds of the field,
That you will not arouse or awaken my love
Until she pleases.
–Song 3:5

But this difficult note leads to one of the most breathtaking parts of the Song. A stunning vision is about to break through the lattice over her soul, even as she continues sleeping restlessly through a veiled night.

Day Twenty:
Fire and Gladness

We often separate "judgment" and "grace," imagining them as opposites. But in the heart of God, they are inseparable—two sides of the same burning love. The deeper we are drawn into his grace-filled kiss, the more we discover its fire. Grace is not passive; it is a sword that cuts through deception and heals with holy precision.

God's judgment is not the rage of an angry tyrant, but the passion of a Lover who will stop at nothing to rescue his stolen bride. He pursues her through the wilderness of her captivity, and when the ransom demands his own life, he offers it without hesitation.

We find this reality of judgment and grace in another part of the Old Testament, in the writings of a prophet named Hosea. God compares Israel to an unfaithful harlot and brings her into a "wilderness" of judgment. But look at what God says about this wilderness:

> *Therefore, behold, I will allure her,*
> *Will bring her into the wilderness,*
> ***And speak comfort to her.***
> –Hosea 2:14 (emphasis mine)

The wilderness now appears in the Shulamite's journey as well. We just saw her leave the boundaries of a city—now we see her leaving the boundaries of the wilderness:

Who is this coming out of the wilderness
Like pillars of smoke,
Perfumed with myrrh and frankincense,
With all the merchant's fragrant powders?
–Song 3:6

The veil, the wall, the bed, and the city all speak to the same issue. They point to a global mindset of spiritual harlotry—the very thing from which God is seeking to rescue the human soul. Now another symbol is thrown into the mix: the wilderness—a place of barrenness and wandering. This is a different image from the others, yet it carries the same meaning.

When God spoke of bringing Israel into the wilderness through Hosea, it marked the culmination of a fiery judgment toward her prostituting ways. Yet it all led to words of comfort—a *kiss*, you might say. From there, the wandering harlot is restored and transformed into a beautiful bride (Hosea 2:15-20).

This brings us back to certain things we saw in the final pages of scripture. When John, the author of Revelation, received the vision of a great harlot, he found her in the wilderness as well. There, she is described as a city engulfed in smoke and flame:

> *So he carried me away in the Spirit into the wilderness. And I saw a woman sitting on a scarlet beast which was full of names of blasphemy... The kings of the earth who committed fornication and lived luxuriously with her will weep and lament for her, when they see the smoke of her burning, standing at a distance for fear of her torment, saying, "Alas, alas, that great city Babylon, that mighty city! For in one hour your judgment has come." And the merchants of the earth will weep and mourn over her...*
> –Revelation 17:3; 18:9-11

The dramatic vision of judgment in the wilderness is then followed by the emergence of a different city—a bridal city

(Revelation 21-22). It's not hard to see that the destruction of Babylon by fire is a picture of humanity's harlotry being judged in the flames of love. But this is to *unveil* our true identity and original blessing—the beloved bride hiding behind her wall.

The King's Carriage

In this part of the Song of Songs, we find the Shulamite out in the wilderness. Still learning to come away from her wall of fear, she wanders through this barren place and looks out into the distance. As she looks, she begins to see something extraordinary—something that connects many more dots throughout the written word of God.

As we read the poetry, the first thing we see is a cloud of fragrant smoke. It's as though a bomb has gone off in a marketplace and all the merchants' spices have been blasted into the air. But as the smoke clears, something else comes forth:

Behold, it is Solomon's couch,
With sixty valiant men around it,
Of the valiant of Israel.
–Song 3:7

Though this translation calls it a "couch," it is really a palanquin—one of those covered carriages that held ancient kings and were carried by poles on the shoulders of servants. The symbolism here is rich and plentiful, but we'll go straight to the heart of the message by looking at the ninth verse:

*The king made this **mercy seat** for himself*
out of the finest wood that will not decay.
–Song 3:9 TPT (emphasis mine)

It turns out the Shulamite is seeing a vision of the Ark of the Covenant—a sacred box that held key artifacts from Israel's journey through the wilderness into the Promised Land (Exodus 25). Its most distinguishing feature was its cover, known as the *mercy seat*.

In reality, this Ark was Yahweh's palanquin. As the true King of Israel, God's presence was enthroned upon this royal mercy seat, carried on poles by priestly servants. Each year, it was stained with blood so that the nation's prostituting sins might be forgiven (Leviticus 16). This annual act—along with the word *covenant* in its title—pointed ahead to the new covenant of Jesus, when the promised Savior would pour out a flood of mercy upon humanity, exchanging his life for our darkness.

Now think back to the harlot in Revelation. John saw her holding a "cup" filled with abominations (Revelation 17:4). When Jesus came to earth, he was called to drink a terrible cup of judgment on our behalf (Matthew 26:39). As he entered the wilderness of our death, he was also clothed in a scarlet robe—the same color as the beast the harlot rode upon. Furthermore, Jesus was surrounded by sword-wielding soldiers who marched him up Calvary's hill after he was publicly branded a blasphemer—a title that rightly belonged to the great harlot.

All these details from Jesus's suffering connect to the vision of Revelation, as well as to the imagery hidden in Solomon's Song. The mystery here is that Jesus took upon himself our beastly, prostituting identity. In his mercy, Christ carried all our brokenness to the cross to restore our true nature. This is what fills the Shulamite's eyes in this section of the Song, and it is sealed by the chapter's final words:

Fire and Gladness

Go forth, O daughters of Zion,
And see King Solomon with the crown
With which his mother crowned him
On the day of his wedding,
The day of the gladness of his heart.
–Song 3:11

On that fateful day of his suffering, Jesus also bore a crown. His "mother"—the nation of Israel, who had painfully carried the promise of a Savior like a child in the womb—crowned Jesus with thorns. So, even though Solomon's poem seems to describe a joyful wedding, it paints a vivid portrait of Jesus's crucifixion.

Of course, it *was* a joyful day—a Good Friday, as we now call it. For Jesus endured the cross "for the joy set before him" (Hebrews 12:2). He did so to bring about the destruction of the veil that blinded our eyes and perverted our paths. Jesus suffered to redeem the person behind the veil—one who was not only a child of the Creator but also a perfect counterpart to the Son of God, like a bride to her bridegroom.

We see this hidden in the book of Genesis through Adam and Eve. In the story, Adam's bride emerges from within him—from the very bones surrounding his heart—and he is overcome with joy: "This is now bone of my bone, and flesh of my flesh!" (Genesis 2:23). This unique and perfect partner for Adam foreshadows humanity's identity before Christ—the "dove" identity hidden by our deceptive veil.

Therefore, this moment in the Song truly depicts "the day of his wedding, the day of the gladness of his heart." At the cross, Jesus was redeeming humankind's bridal status. It was indeed a day of great joy in his heart, even though it looked quite the opposite.

The Kiss of Christ

Moreover, when Jesus uttered his final words—*"It is finished"*—the prophetic vision of John came true: *"In one hour, her destruction came."*

Swiftly, God laid his fiery judgment upon the false self. With blazing grace, Jesus forgave our participation in darkness and separated us from its claim. "For in the Son all our sins are canceled," wrote Paul, "and we have the release of redemption through his very blood" (Colossians 1:14 TPT).

The true bride was always there, hidden behind a veil of deception. In loving judgment, Christ put away that beastly veil by taking it upon his own body and carrying it into the grave. At the same time, the veil in Solomon's temple was torn—a sign that the universal veil over humanity had been destroyed. In that moment, our true identity as the beloved counterpart to God's Son was restored.

Such is the meaning of this strange vision in Solomon's Song where we see a palanquin—the true mercy seat—emerging from the wilderness. It is a picture of God's suffering love for his beloved bride. The great Shepherd King put us on his shoulders and carried us out of the wilderness of our harlotry.

And now this truth will rise to an unimaginable crescendo in the next words that flow from the King's mouth.

Day Twenty-One:
It is Finished

I used to think the idea of following some resurrected Jewish man—who oversees a rather lame group of religious people called Christians—was laughable. I told people it would take an absolute miracle for someone like me to believe. Thank God, that miracle came. My heart opened to the truth. Faith cracked a shell around my mind and brought a tide of healing with it.

To this day, I believe it takes a work of complete grace to open the heart to the mysteries of God. In fact, more grace is needed as we go further into who he is and what he says about us.

With that said, grace beyond imagining is needed to take in what we're about to discover...

A Sevenfold Declaration

We've joined the "daughters of Zion" in beholding the Man crowned with thorns—the One rising from the desert of death, carrying his bride with him. Now we must tune our ears to listen more closely, for unimaginable words begin to pour from his mouth. Words that should make us pause and ask for divine help to take in even a portion of their truth.

In the first seven verses of Song of Songs 4, we find the King praising seven aspects of the Shulamite. The first verse begins by calling her beautiful. He does this twice, establishing a double confirmation of her identity as one who bears the image of the perfect One.

How beautiful you are, my darling,
How beautiful you are! ...

He then follows up with this familiar imagery:

... Your eyes are like doves behind your veil.

In case there's any doubt about the biblical connection between the prostitute and the bride, here's an important note: outside of Solomon's Song, the Hebrew word for *veil* appears only once in scripture—in a passage pronouncing judgment on Babylon. God says to the wicked city, *"Remove your veil"* (Isaiah 47:2). Remarkably, that same chapter is quoted by the apostle John when he describes the judgment coming to the harlot city in Revelation 18:7.

The Shulamite is truly wearing the veil of Babylon—yet we're discovering that Jesus looks right through it and declares her a perfect reflection of his life and Spirit. Her eyes are like doves!

Now let's recall the broader context of the Song. We've seen the Son of God crowned with thorns on the day of his wedding—the day of the new covenant. In this moment, he's speaking *from that place*. In other words, this is a poetic image of him rising from the wilderness of death, proclaiming the truth of our redemption.

He goes on to speak of other aspects of the Shulamite—her hair, symbolizing wisdom and dedication; her teeth, symbolizing the ability to chew on and understand the word of God. Each feature is rich in meaning, though beyond the scope of this book to fully unpack. So we'll jump ahead to the summative statement in the seventh verse:

You are altogether beautiful, my darling,
And there is no blemish in you.
–Song 4:7

It is Finished

The truth of her beauty is sealed with a third witness. This time, the meaning of his words is unmistakable: she is altogether beautiful and without any imperfection!

In this unfolding scene of Christ's death and resurrection, the Shulamite is being called *perfect*. This offers a glimpse into the heart of God when, on the cross, the Son took away our veiling shame and made a timeless declaration:

> *Therefore when Jesus had received the sour wine, He said, "It is finished!" And He bowed His head and gave up His spirit.*
> –John 19:30

As noted, the King describes seven features of the Shulamite before proclaiming her perfection. This is fitting, since seven is the biblical number of completion. It was on the seventh day God finished the work of creation and rested—celebrating its completed beauty. That seventh day foreshadowed the day Christ would complete the new creation and rest from this redemptive act—celebrating, once again, the beauty of a finished work.

The Mystery of Kalah

It is likely that when Jesus cried out the words, *"It is finished,"* he spoke in the language of his people—Aramaic. The scriptures even preserve one of his Aramaic utterances directly (Matthew 27:46). Aramaic, a sister language to Hebrew, holds a powerful mystery in the phrase *"It is finished."* It is translated from the word *kalah*, which speaks of something being completed.

However, *kalah* also carries another meaning.

It is the word for "bride." Such is the reason Jesus's final words are rendered in The Passion Translation as follows:

The Kiss of Christ

When he had sipped the sour wine, he said, "It is finished, my bride!"
–John 19:30 TPT

It's remarkable how this single word captures both meanings. Jesus is celebrating the beauty of his redeemed bride as he completes the work of canceling her sin!

Even more amazing is the way this connects with the Song of Songs. Immediately after the King says the Shulamite is altogether beautiful and without blemish, he declares:

*Come with me from Lebanon, my **bride**...*

Or, in the original tongue:

*Come with me from Lebanon, my **kalah**.*

Truly, the Song offers a vision of Christ's kiss awakening our veiled and sleeping hearts. Jesus entered our self-induced wilderness to destroy it from the inside out. He took our shame and replaced it with his righteousness. As we've seen, this is him redeeming—buying back—the original blessing that was always ours, yet locked away under a spell of deception.

Now look at the verse preceding those poetic words of the Shulamite's perfection. Before he makes that proclamation, the King says:

Until the day breaks
And the shadows flee away,
I will go my way to the mountain of myrrh
And to the hill of frankincense.
–Song 4:6 NKJV

You may recall the Shulamite's earlier words, when she told the King to turn away. She said she would not come away with him *"until the day breaks and the shadows flee away."* She also described him standing on the mountain of Bether—*separation*.

Now the Lord responds. He agrees that the new day hasn't fully come. Shadows still linger over the earth—and over her own heart. But that's where the agreement ends. He goes on to say that he is standing on a different mountain—not one of separation, but of *myrrh* and *frankincense*, two symbols we've explored before. Do you remember their meaning?

They are symbols of death and resurrection.

In other words, the Lord is declaring that even though his Kingdom has not fully manifested on earth, he still stands victorious on a very specific mountain—the mountain of Calvary, the place where his work of a new creation was finished. And from that mountain, he declares with joy and conviction:

"You are altogether perfect!"

From heaven's vantage point, this is now the truth over our lives.

And this is the kiss of eternity—the sword of God's word that splits the sky and tears through the Babylonian veil that has plagued the world.

This is what we need grace to receive.

Which is why it's the perfect time for another *selah*.

Selah

At the beginning of our journey, we peered into space through the eyes of a giant telescope and beheld an array of galaxies. We learned that this unimaginable army of galactic structures was contained in just one small speck of the night sky.

Such a thought has the power to humble us—a reminder that our minds are frail and cannot even begin to comprehend the depths of creation.

The same holds true for the images found in the written word, especially in this little poem occupying a small speck of the Bible. It should remind us that we cannot even begin to understand the depths of the *new creation*.

This is why the apostle Paul wrote of our need for divine strength and power.

For a moment, let's pause and pray with him again:

So I kneel humbly in awe before the Father of our Lord Jesus, the Messiah, the perfect Father of every father and child in heaven and on the earth.

And I pray that he would unveil within you the unlimited riches of his glory and favor until supernatural strength floods your innermost being with his divine might and explosive power...

Then you will be empowered to discover what every holy one experiences—the great magnitude of the astonishing

love of Christ in all its dimensions. How deeply intimate and far-reaching is his love! How enduring and inclusive it is! Endless love beyond measurement that transcends our understanding—this extravagant love pours into you until you are filled to overflowing with the fullness of God!
–Ephesians 3:16, 18-19 TPT–

Movement Four

Harmony

Day Twenty-Two:
The Vulnerability of God

When the true Gospel goes into the human ear and settles down into the heart, a bomb goes off. As the message of Jesus's life, death, and resurrection reaches a place of true understanding, wonder and joy are released like a mushroom cloud, saturating the atmosphere of our soul and forever changing its landscape.

Sadly, the explosive ingredients of this message are often diluted—or sometimes completely removed before they arrive at their target. When delivered, they end up as a dud or, at best, cause a small explosion that leaves a temporary crater but doesn't shift our interior world.

The Song of Solomon, with its symbolic foreshadowing, offers us a precious gift: it helps recover the potency of the Gospel. Among its treasures is a fuller understanding of the sin covering humanity—likened to a prostitute's veil that hides our true face. God has come to cut down this veil with a sword of light: the truth revealed and redeemed in Christ's work on the cross. The Shulamite was given a vision of this as she witnessed swift judgment coming upon our darkness, along with a corresponding affirmation of our true value.

In the aftermath of this vision, the King's words lead us straight into the "why" behind the Gospel. Countless theological propositions have been offered to explain the purpose of Jesus's death, but none speak with the simplicity and power of what we find here—words later echoed in the New Testament by the apostle John:

The Kiss of Christ

For God so loved the world that he gave his one and only Son...
–John 3:16 NIV

According to John, love was the reason for his death.

Yet these famous words are often watered down, losing their combustible power. And so Solomon comes to our aid, helping us see more clearly what drove the Son of God to descend from heaven, down the ladder of DNA, so that he could one day ascend the hill of Calvary.

In our search for revelation beneath the dirt of earthly images—mountains, deserts, tables—our shovels have struck gold. This next passage leads us to the jackpot. Let's take our time and read it from a few translations...

> *You have stolen my heart, my sister, my bride;*
> *you have stolen my heart with one glance of your eyes...*
> –Song 4:9 NIV

> *You have ravished my heart,*
> *My sister, my spouse;*
> *You have ravished my heart*
> *With one look of your eyes...*
> –NKJV

> *For you reach into my heart.*
> *With one flash of your eyes I am undone by your love,*
> *my beloved, my equal, my bride.*
> *You leave me breathless—I am overcome*
> *by merely a glance from your worshiping eyes,*
> *for you have stolen my heart.*
> *I am held hostage by your love*
> *and by the graces of righteousness shining upon you.*
> –TPT

Each translation attempts to describe what this Shulamite woman does to the heart of King Solomon. She is said to "ravish" his heart ... "steal" it ... "undo" it ... "hold it hostage" ...

These dramatic expressions are not exaggerations of the Hebrew. The poem speaks of his heart being undeniably impacted by another. His heart rate rises just thinking about her! His focus and attention—the eyes of his heart—are held captive by her beauty and persona. He fixes this passionate gaze on her and longs for her friendship and well-being.

The Agapè God

But there's even more to discover when we look closer at the word being translated in these dramatic ways. The term rendered as "ravished" comes from a root word that describes the tearing of bark from a tree. When the protective covering is removed, a tree becomes vulnerable to the elements. Without bark, it's exposed—and in danger of death.

If God so loved the world *like this* ... suddenly the Gospel makes a lot of sense.

With an intense passion to rescue us from captivity, God entered the world in the most vulnerable state imaginable: a helpless infant. God gave himself completely into our hands—literally, into the hands of Eve's descendant, Mary. Then, at the end of his life, we find God naked once again before his mother, hanging from a Roman execution stake, all protective covering gone.

The glory of God is often depicted with imagery of clouds, fire, and lightning. But at the cross, we learn that all of that was like bark around a tree. Behind those glorious displays of power is a tenderness we cannot fathom. As Jesus was killed, the true glory of God—the Holy of Holies of his being—was unveiled before our eyes. With arms spread wide and heart fully exposed, God cried out words of unquenchable lovingkindness.

These depths in the heart of God are described by one of the Greek terms for love—*agapè*. "God is *agapè*," the apostle John wrote elsewhere. Fittingly, he's the one who rested his head on Jesus's chest, tuning his ear to the rhythm of that ravished heart (John 13:23). John was also the only disciple to witness what happened at the tree of Calvary the next day.

God's Own Promised Land

Do you remember how we said at the beginning of our journey that revelation is the currency of heaven? That's what kickstarted our scavenger hunt through the cosmos, scripture, and human life in search of this illuminating treasure. What we've discovered is that the entire Song is a *revelation* of what we do to God's heart. We are tapping into heavenly treasure when we realize that God looks at the human soul and is overcome by a glorious desire for our restoration and safety.

And many of us don't even need this map of Solomon's Song to locate this treasure. Some find it etched on the map of our own lives—in the fierce and tender love we feel for our children.

But here's an important question: What is it about the Shulamite—*the human soul*—that drives the Lord into such a display of vulnerable love?

We find more clues as we keep reading. Besides calling her his *kalah*, the King addresses the Shulamite as his "sister." This opens up a world of truth about our familial bond to Jesus. A brother and sister share the same origin and likeness. They come from the same home and have the same nature.

Yes, God's own beauty is reflected in us, and this causes an otherworldly love to erupt in his heart as he watches our unique lives play out. A piece of him resides within us. It's like what a parent feels when looking into the eyes of their child—seeing someone who is precious and unique, someone who carries their very image.

We find this confirmed when the King begins to speak of the "garden" of the Shulamite. Solomon describes nine spices, or "fruits," which interestingly align with the nine fruits of the Holy Spirit described in the New Testament (see Song 4:12-15 and Galatians 5:22-23). He also makes this stunning statement:

Your lips, my bride, drip honey;
Honey and milk are under your tongue...
–Song 4:11

Honey and milk are consistently associated with the Promised Land in scripture (Exodus 3:8). By describing her inner life this way, we learn that *we* are God's own Promised Land! The entire universe was fine-tuned for a garden to emerge—and that garden is not a place, but a people. This is the center of creation, and it's what drove the heart of the Creator to suffer on earth at a specific time and place in order to redeem it.

As we peer into the wonders of this chapter, we're stepping into our royal calling as treasure hunters. From the opening lines, we've journeyed deeper and deeper into this gold mine—sitting at the King's table, dining in the house of wine, riding the carriage through the wilderness, and now listening to the stunning words of passion from the mouth of our crowned King.

These words reflect the greatest theology ever discovered. They're so good they had to be buried like treasure in an ancient love poem—and, as we've seen, they're also buried in the dust of our human relationships.

The Kiss of Christ

Of course, this is more than theology in the academic sense. This is verifiable history in the life, death, and resurrection of the Messiah, Jesus of Nazareth. This love appeared in tangible form. It went to a real cross and emerged from a real grave in Israel.

This is a treasure we can take to the bank of our hearts—and then watch as it detonates with transformative force.

Day Twenty-Three: Communion and the Door

The fifth chapter of the eternal Song of Solomon begins like this:

I have come into my garden, my sister, my bride;
I have gathered my myrrh along with my balsam.
I have eaten my honeycomb and my honey;
I have drunk my wine and my milk.
Eat, friends;
Drink and imbibe deeply, O lovers.
—Song 5:1

We've gone searching for treasure but ended up stumbling upon a rich banquet. Everything revealed in the Shulamite's journey has become a meal that satisfies every craving of the heart. The truth of our origin, along with the mystery of what lies in the depths of God's heart—these revelations are a feast for the soul, both intoxicating and nourishing at the same time.

In the above passage, the King tells the Shulamite that he is within her garden. His life abides inside her. There is no greater message than this. Like food to the body, she is called to receive the truth of his loving presence, letting nothing hold her back from allowing his words to define her very existence.

Nevertheless, the Shulamite has not yet taken in the full meal set before her. According to the next verse, we find her still asleep. She is on her bed, presumably hiding behind that same veiling wall from before. *"I was asleep but my heart was awake,"* she says. Still, she is in a dream state.

The Kiss of Christ

And so the King continues to call to her:

A voice! My beloved was knocking:
"Open to me, my sister, my darling,
My dove, my perfect one!
For my head is drenched with dew,
My locks with the damp of the night."
–Song 5:2

With each knock on her sleeping heart, the Lord seeks to awaken his bride to all that has been revealed to her. His knock is the same as his earlier call. It is the invitation to "come away" and "arise" from the slumber of separation and fear. He continues to release the kisses of his word—the very thing she asked for at the beginning of her journey.

This kiss now comes to her in the form of four simple titles: *Sister, darling, dove, perfect one.*

He tells her—actually, let's personalize it—*he tells you, beloved reader:*

You are my holy sibling. You belong in my home, for it is your home as well. You are part of the Divine Family.

You are my darling treasure. You move my heart with unimaginable passion and desire.

You are my dove. Precious and innocent, I compare you to my own Spirit.

You are perfect. You are complete in my sight—whole and true. You lack nothing.

As he speaks these tremendous words, summarizing all that has been revealed up to this point, we see his head drenched with *"the damp of the night."* Christ is speaking here from the aftermath of his suffering, when he was crowned with thorns and tore down the veil of our false identity. Ever since the Shulamite came to the table and experienced a vision of the cross, this same melody has continued to play. Now Jesus stands before her and calls her to awaken from the discord and enter the victorious sound of his grace.

And thank God—she responds. In the next verse, she confesses that she has taken off her old garments and washed her dirty feet. She agrees with the truth that she is made as clean as a sacrificial dove. This is why we see her getting out of bed in verse 5, and why these words come out of her mouth:

> *...my hands dripped with myrrh*
> *And my fingers with liquid myrrh,*
> *On the handles of the bolt.*
> –Song 5:5

The Shulamite is taking hold of the cross for herself. Her hands dripping with myrrh show her engaging with the reality of Jesus's suffering. Everything he has spoken to her is now in her hands—a picture of her taking ownership of it.

Right here, we are witnessing the act of communion. This is what opens the hard "bolt" over the door of her heart and takes her into heaven's riches. It is what the Lord desired for her from the beginning, and we see the same thing echoed in the book of Revelation, where Jesus speaks to his bride:

> *Behold, I'm standing at the door, knocking. If your heart is open to hear my voice and you open the door within, I will come in to you and feast with you, and you will feast with me.*
> –Revelation 3:20 TPT

Jesus longs for us to welcome the kiss of his redeeming truth. This word—revealed and established at the cross—is the only thing that can awaken the human soul and cause the garden within to blossom.

The Shulamite is answering this call. She is rising from her bed and opening the door. With this, she moves into a completely new season of life.

Day Twenty-Four: The Mystery and Tension

As I write this book, I keep getting drawn back to my time in Asia. Part of the reason, I believe, is that my spirit is celebrating the banner of Christ's love that is destined to unfold over that spiritually war-torn continent. Yet what comes to mind now is a moment when I was able to worship with other brothers and sisters of Jesus who were singing in a language I didn't understand.

We were in a secretive location in the capital city of the nation, celebrating the glory of Christ together. Despite the verbal barrier, my heart melted with each word as I joined in silent praise exuding from the center of my being. I remember the tears streaming down our faces as we worshipped together in that place.

In that moment, I saw how the Song of the Lamb—the Song written into the cosmos from all eternity and now coursing its way through human history—can never be repressed. It transcends every religious boundary and breaks down every cultural wall. Just one encounter with Jesus will ignite this Song on the inside. No matter where you are, or what human language is being uttered, nothing can stop it from spilling out—even under intense resistance.

A Cold, Dark Night

After hearing many lyrics from this Song of all songs, the Shulamite is finally starting to believe it. She opens the door of her heart and steps out in trust. Unfortunately, soon after she does, something happens that causes her to slip back into a place of discord.

The Shulamite opens her heart to the loving truth of Jesus, but finds a cold, dark night in front of her…

> *I opened to my beloved,*
> *But my beloved had turned away and had gone!*
> *My heart went out to him as he spoke.*
> *I searched for him but I did not find him;*
> *I called him but he did not answer me.*
> –Song 5:6

The Shulamite embraces Jesus's words, but she goes on to experience *contradiction*. She looks out and sees a world still caught in unbelief. Pain and suffering are still in her purview. Hatred and division lurk in nearby alleyways. Conspiracy and fear hang from twisted branches off of cursed family trees. Persecution is at the doorstep as well.

In other words, that wondrous springtime the Shepherd promised earlier seems a million miles away. In fact, the resurrected King appears to be missing as well. But it is here we come to the great mystery and tension of faith. It's imperative we stop and gain some understanding from this part of the journey, especially if we want to take hold of the riches we've uncovered so far.

Hope Against Hope

In this scene, the Shulamite is being tempted to filter her treasured revelation through what she sees and feels. The problem is that she is not yet accustomed to this new realm called *trust*. She must learn to walk in what the scriptures call "hope against hope" (Romans 4:18).

The Mystery and Tension

This phrase is made in connection to Abraham, the one who is known as the forefather of faith. *Abram* was kissed by God with a wild promise and given the new identity of Abraham—"the father of many nations." Abraham opened the door of his heart to trust in this incredible word, yet immediately found himself in a contradictory waiting period. He was the furthest thing from a father of nations, and because of this, he entered a lingering battle with trust. Along the way, he experienced many setbacks and a few personal failures as well.

Despite this, a gracious account of his life is written into the New Testament. Paul declares that he walked "in hope against hope" and eventually experienced what was promised. Though Abraham stumbled, he did not fall into full agreement with unbelief. He lived out the tension of faith and went on to encounter wonderful things.

So it is with the Shulamite. She is now in her own battle of trust. For this reason, we find her stumbling back into old lies. She declares, *"My beloved had turned away and had gone!"* The One who promised to never leave her nor forsake her is now being accused of abandonment.

From here, the Shulamite is thrust into a series of difficult circumstances. Sadly, she returns to the city of religion in search of God's presence. In this case, however, she encounters even greater resistance, as her interactions with the watchmen leave her badly wounded this time around.

In all of this, she finds herself wrestling with a demonic kiss—a word from hell that speaks the exact opposite of the word of original blessing. It is the word *rejection*.

The Kiss of Christ

The Moment of Turning

Yet she refuses to give up. This young maiden from Shulam has experienced too much to dismiss the promises of Jesus. She may question God's intentions—and his location—but the longing for his presence has not left her.

Because of this, the Shulamite asks for help from those around her, even from those who are less spiritually experienced. These are the daughters of Jerusalem, the onlookers of the story who now reenter the poetry. She turns to them and essentially asks for guidance on how to find God (v. 8). There is a sense of humility here, yet it is mixed with her spiritual forgetfulness and doubt.

The daughters do not know where this Shepherd King is, but their interest is piqued when they see the passion within her. They want to know why he is so special to her, and to this the Shulamite responds with a poetic stream of words. Words that contain some of the most beautiful truths about Jesus ever penned. Truths that continue to hide behind ancient allegory.

She begins with the following:

My beloved is dazzling and ruddy,
Outstanding among ten thousand.
–Song 5:10

As we dig further into these words, we first find a hidden message about the nature of Christ. The word *dazzling* is used for a brilliant, shining light—a concept biblically associated with heavenly realities. *Ruddy*, on the other hand, comes from the root word for *Adam*. It can be translated as red or earthy. These two terms—*dazzling* and *ruddy*—speak to the divinity and humanity of Jesus.

The Mystery and Tension

What's happening is that the Shulamite is returning to the basics of her faith. She is reminded of the cornerstone of everything—the truth that Jesus is fully human and yet shines with divine glory. He is outstanding among all others, including every prophet and teacher who has come before or after him. Truly, he is the Creator of time and space, and he dwells in human flesh. She declares that this is the Beloved of her story—the One who adores and pursues her soul.

From here, the Song of the Lamb begins to rise from the ashes of her trials. Words of praise continue to pour from her mouth as she utters mystery upon mystery about Christ's nature. Before long, the Shulamite moves from descriptions of his head to exclamations over other features of his body. Part by part, she releases her celebration and awe over Christ's personhood—until she finally arrives at the feet. Then something happens.

A shift occurs in her heart.

And with this shift comes the greatest surprise of the Song—something that will crystallize all that came before into one piercing note.

Twenty-Five:
Crescendo of the Song

In the midst of sorrow and doubt, a simple question led the Shulamite to a golden opportunity—the opportunity to turn her eyes away from herself.

When the daughters asked for the identity of her Beloved, something began to shift in her perception. As she turned her focus back to the goodness of God, a realization emerged. She came to a stunning conclusion, one that will become clear as she begins to wrap up her triumphant poetry about the King.

> *His mouth is sweetness itself;*
> *He is altogether lovely.*
> *This is my beloved, this is my friend,*
> *Daughters of Jerusalem.*
> –Song 5:16 NIV

After describing his entire being, the Shulamite concludes by returning to a very particular feature of his body: she speaks of the King's *"mouth."* This detail is significant, as it brings us back to the beginning of her story. When we first met the Shulamite, she was striving under the heat of religion and made a bold request to God—she asked for the kisses of his mouth.

The kisses of revelation began to flow, reminding her of the original blessing that still lay inside of her. This blessing of complete acceptance and perfect identity was always there, yet it remained hidden behind a veil of fear and unbelief.

By recalling the mouth—the vehicle through which his word flows—the Shulamite comes back to this truth as she concludes her celebration of the King. She calls this vehicle *"sweetness itself."* Indeed, the Gospel—the kiss of eternal grace flowing from God's mouth—is the essence of all goodness. There is no better message, no sweeter truth, no higher philosophy or spiritual path. Though she has weathered many conflicting storms, the Shulamite knows that nothing compares to this word of truth.

In fact, when a person doesn't give up, the storms around them only solidify this truth. The Shulamite discovered this for herself as she pressed through the resistance with gratitude and returned to the place of communion. The wounds of the watchmen may still sting, and the clamor of a dark world may still bite at her, but fresh light has broken through the pain. Now, the essence of the Song fills her own mouth.

As she rises up with the word of grace, the Shulamite adds to her celebration of the Beloved: *"He is altogether lovely!"*

This statement takes us back to the core revelation of the Song—a truth we unearthed earlier when we struck the motherlode of gold in the finale of the third movement. There, this same declaration came from the King's mouth toward her.

Something has clicked inside her, and it will be fully revealed in the next chapter of the Song when the daughters of Jerusalem ask this follow-up question:

> *Where has your beloved gone...?*
> –Song 6:1

Remembering the Mystery

As they listen to her speak these beautiful words of praise, something is ignited within these onlookers. The Song is contagious! The daughters of Jerusalem have a desire awakened in them, and so they ask the Shulamite where they might find this amazing Creator who is also a sweet Lover and Friend.

Because she turned her eyes away from herself and entered the place of praise and remembrance, the Shulamite is led back to a forgotten truth. The sweetness of his word—the sweetest, most precious message ever spoken—has returned to her awareness. She remembers his kiss of truth and answers their question with fiery clarity, revealing the truth that has finally broken through her soul:

> *My beloved has gone down to his garden,*
> *To the beds of balsam,*
> *To pasture his flock in the gardens*
> *And gather lilies;*
> *I am my beloved's and my beloved is mine...*
> –Song 6:2-3

This answer is more glorious and spiritually significant than we can imagine. The Shulamite—a picture of the rising human soul—has come to accept something she has been subtly (and sometimes overtly) resisting: she realizes her Beloved *never* turned away and left her.

The lingering darkness she experienced—when she opened the door of her heart and stepped into a world with only a handful of communion elements—did not cancel his promise.

Her own struggles and doubts did not negate his word either.

Where was he, then? Where was he during the pain? Where was he in the persecution? Where was he in the place of prayer and struggle and doubt and questioning?

My Beloved is within his garden, she says.

Do you remember what—or who—the garden is?

Yes, the Beloved has been *within her* the whole time. She is the promised garden of God, as we learned in the first part of this movement. Her heart is truly the home of triune glory and friendship.

The human soul—the Shulamite—is the house of the Almighty, the place scripture calls Bethel: "house of God" in Hebrew. Bethel is where Abraham's grandson laid his head and experienced a vision of a heavenly ladder touching down upon the earth (Genesis 28).

We've alluded to this ladder before when we spoke of the foundation of human blood and the shape of DNA as a kind of spiraling ladder. It is not a far stretch to describe this as the pathway God descended into the world through the physical womb of Mary.

But Christ did not come for only a singular body. This is what the Shulamite came to understand as she moved from describing his glorious headship down to his feet. As she reflected on each part of his being, she began to remember that his body includes us. We are his temple! We are altogether lovely because we are united to the One who is altogether lovely.

This was the sweet word that returned to her heart. And this is what leads her to this great conclusion—the crystallizing note of the whole Song: *"I am my Beloved's and my Beloved is mine!"*

As the Shulamite celebrates the truth of her unbreakable union with Christ, we enter the crescendo of the music. In spite of what she has seen and felt—including all the pain that struck her heart from the religious systems around her—she is now moving forward and looking beyond the world's limited horizon.

Crescendo of the Song

Now nothing will be able to stop the flow of this music. The awakened soul knows that its dusty frame, weak as it may be, is a container of glory—a glory filled with perfect love. Love that will never leave us nor forsake us. He eternally dwells within, and this is, in fact, the mystery hidden in all things. Even behind the worst kinds of prostituting veils, this mystery abides.

Every veil, no matter how dark, is a lie.

And all of it is washed under the blood of the Lamb. For Christ is the "Passover Lamb" of scripture. He is the One who passed over the sin of the world and declared the truth of our original beauty. He now calls each and every person to awake and arise to this same blessing.

Despite what anyone else says, the Shulamite has taken hold of this treasure and will not let go. Because of this, everything around her will begin to change.

Twenty-Six: When the Light Dawns

There's a special spot in my neighborhood where I secretly covet a small stretch of houses. They offer a particular view of the highlands of northern New Jersey, where there's a stunning display of light as the sun washes over the mountains.

It's remarkable what happens when light breaks in on a scene like this. Entire mountains that were invisible during the night suddenly emerge like hidden guardians along the horizon. You might be able to see faint traces of their outline during the night, but their color and contours—their sprawling forestry or snowy drapery—remain veiled until the dawn rolls in. Then, everything comes into focus. A new world of exploration opens before you, with rising trails and hidden habitats. And yet nothing has actually changed. Light has simply exposed what was hidden and sleeping.

It is the same with revelation. When the light of truth dawns upon the soul, new territory opens up. In the morning of spiritual understanding, new sights emerge and sleeping things awake. Nothing has changed, and yet everything changes.

One of the changes is that people around you begin to take notice. Just as rising sunlight can transform a dark stretch of clouds and cause onlookers to be captivated by the sight, so it is with the revelation-infused believer. This is what happens with the Shulamite as her story reaches its crescendo and she lays hold of the treasure she has found.

The Shulamite has been awakened—and now begins to manifest what was previously hidden. In hope against hope, her heart stayed true to her Beloved's kiss. Now, she begins to bear the fruit of God's life within her. Like Abraham's wife, who bore a supernatural child named Laughter (the meaning of Isaac in Hebrew), the Shulamite begins to exude divine joy. Such an attractive and sweet fruit catches the attention of those around her, as we see in the following words:

...The maidens saw her and called her blessed,
The queens and concubines also, and they praised her, saying,
"Who is this that grows like the dawn,
As beautiful as the full moon,
As pure as the sun,
As awesome as an army with banners?"
*–*Song 6:10 (emphasis mine)

The True Church

The maidens, queens, and concubines represent those who do not yet intimately know the King of glory. They may be in some kind of relationship or proximity to him, but they have not awakened to the full mystery of Christ. They do not know what it means to be consumed by his love.

Yet something in the life of the Shulamite causes them to compare her to the dawn. Like the almond tree signaling the coming of spring, the Shulamite heralds the arrival of a new day to a world that is still asleep. This brings us to a deeper understanding of what the scriptures call "the church."

Like tall mountains in the black of night, the true church has been hidden in darkness for much of its history. Though some crude outlines can be seen in this night season of humanity, the full wonders of the church have not yet appeared.

Praising her beauty, the Shulamite's observers go on to compare her to a full moon—another fitting metaphor given everything we've explored. The moon does not generate light of its own; it simply turns toward the sun and reflects its glory onto the earth. And such is the church's calling: to reflect the light of Christ to a world still sleeping under a deceptive veil. Yet, like the moon's hard exterior, the church often appears like a dusty group of people, dry and dotted with empty craters.

Even so, we are positioned in the heavenly realm in such a way that we're able to catch beams of divine grace and pass them on to others. For much of her history, the church has done this only in part. Like a crescent moon, her light has appeared in slivers—waxing and waning through seasons of history. But the time is coming when the church will be fully aligned with her Bridegroom's light, shining with the fullness of his glory, bathed in the starlight of grace.

And this sets us up for what is spoken next about the rising Shulamite.

Glad Tidings of Great Joy

> *How beautiful are your feet in sandals,*
> *O prince's daughter! ...*
> –Song 7:1

"Beautiful feet" echoes a phrase from the prophet Isaiah, used to describe those who carry good news to others (Isaiah 52:7). In other words, this poetic statement is about evangelism. Like the word church, *evangelism* is a term that's been dragged through the religious mud over the years, losing much of its original beauty. But the beauty can be recovered—especially if we return to the original context of this phrase.

Without social media or radio, news in ancient times had to travel by the physical mouth of messengers. A person with beautiful feet was one appointed to run across hills and plains into secluded villages and cities with wonderful news. Often, this news was about a military victory. Arriving breathless in the center of a town, such a runner would declare something like this:

Our king's armies have defeated the barbarian forces at our border! The enemy who threatened to overthrow our towns, kill our men, and kidnap our women and children is no more. The threat is gone. You can relax and celebrate!

Surely, for a community riddled with anxiety over an uncertain future, such a messenger would come running with the most beautiful feet imaginable. These glad and welcoming feet would spark a flurry of parties and celebrations, especially among those who believed the message—even if they didn't see the victory with their own eyes.

This brings us back to the explosive power of the Gospel. We're beginning to see how the Shulamite is destined to carry this message with its powerful and intoxicating truths to the world around her. Having drunk the wine of grace herself, she is now ready to bring this drink to others. For she runs with the key that unlocks the human soul's potential. This key is found in the kiss of God—the message of pure and absolute grace.

It is the Word of Jesus Christ, of his death and resurrection.

Death is defeated. Guilt has been drowned in the grave. We are now raised to new life through the work of our divine Representative.

With this, the Shulamite carries a message of glad tidings and great joy. Through her own story—what we might call her testimony—she has discovered that even when you feel forsaken, the King has never left you. He is Immanuel. God with us.

He is here, all around us, and his heart beats with a tender and precious love.

And that takes us into even more good news: we have a heavenly Father—and he is not angry with us! He longs for us, waiting for us to turn our gaze back to his smile. Indeed, we have an entire family in the home of a good and happy Trinity. We have a Father's embrace and a Mother's grip, just as we have everlasting Brotherhood in the person of Jesus.

In other words, the original blessing of Eden still holds true. We are blessed beyond imagination. This blessing simply waits for our hearts to open wide to receive it like a Lover's kiss—a kiss that wakes us from the lying spell that says we are rejected and alone.

When we read the words, *"The maidens saw her and called her blessed,"* this is what they were seeing. The original blessing is beginning to radiate from her awakened life. Now she will seek to unleash that blessing upon every person she meets.

Day Twenty-Seven: Our Calling and Destiny

We've been on a search for the treasure of life-changing revelation. We've dug deep into the fabric of creation and down into the pages of scripture, tracking the footsteps of a young woman who captured the heart of a king. Now that this Shulamite is moving into the final stages of her journey, she sums up the beautiful revelation she's discovered:

> *Now I know that I am for my beloved*
> *and all his desires are fulfilled in me.*
> –Song 7:10 TPT

With the Shulamite's help, we've unearthed the most stunning truth imaginable:

We are made *for God*.

And this "God" is not some vague invisible force, nor is he a wrathful religious deity.

He is the Beloved of the Song. He is our Lover and Friend—the One who tore the bark off the exterior of our understanding of him to reveal a tender, beating heart within. He is the crucified Christ who invites us to the table of friendship to drink of his love in the house of wine.

In the beginning, we looked at the origins of space and time, and how our cosmic canopy was mapped out by an eternal relationship known as the Trinity. This Divine Family dreamed of others to include in their love—a love that flowed endlessly, like a song of ecstatic praise. With fresh lyrics rising in their heart, they exhaled and sang out the created order, preparing the way for the chorus that had been building within them.

This new chorus was the emergence of children.

Children who would bring them unthinkable joy.

We are those children who were made specifically for God. We are desired by the entire Trinity. Thus, we too can say with the Shulamite, *"I am for my Beloved, and all his desires are fulfilled in me!"*

To be desired is, in fact, a core desire of the heart. Both men and women carry this yearning to be cherished and admired—to know that One greater than you is proud of you, that One stronger than you is pursuing you, that the perfect One looks into your eyes and sees a perfect reflection of himself.

Such is the treasure of revelation-knowledge we've dug up as we followed the Shulamite to the table of grace. She received this truth as the greatest blessing of all, and now we will find her changing direction, moving with a newfound sense of purpose.

Running with Joy

Come away, my lover.
Come with me to the faraway fields.
We will run away together to the forgotten places
and show them redeeming love.
−Song of 7:11 TPT

Secure in her King's love, the Shulamite's eyes are opened to the needs around her. She desires to go to the lost and forgotten, to reach out to those who are experiencing all the opposites of "blessing"—those living under the throes of poverty, injustice, and grief. Those living under the curse of a false identity.

Our Calling and Destiny

This illuminates another word that's been dragged through the religious mud over the years: *ministry*. Originally, this term had to do with good service—like an excellent waiter who honors and serves the people at their table. Indeed, the church is called to invite the world to a table of fellowship and serve them as excellent "ministers" of good news.

This is meant to be an act of love, not something derived from guilt or religious duty. It arises from joy and divine intimacy. It is the reason Jesus himself went to the forgotten places to serve the poor, the broken, and the hungry.

In light of this, the Shulamite is expressing more of her true nature as an image-bearer. She is reflecting the One who gave birth to humanity out of an already fulfilled relationship. Creation was the overflow of the Trinity's love, and now, as one of their awakened children, she demonstrates this same kind of overflow in her desire to bless others.

And yet she does this not to fill a hole inside herself. She goes because she has discovered that the hole was a lie! She now wants others to discover this same treasure of revelation for themselves.

From the start, the Shulamite felt this call to be a "runner" of good news. We saw this after her initial request for the kiss of life, when she cried out, *"Draw me after you and let us run together!"* (Song 1:4).

This purpose lay deep inside of her, and it dwells within every single person reading these words. As a symbol of the human soul, the Shulamite has unique gifts and passions placed within her, and these arise from the mission to partner with our Creator in beautifying the world.

Yet for the Shulamite—and us—there was a religious wall blocking this calling from coming out in a healthy way. Though she wanted to help others, the Shepherd's priority was to first bring her to the table where she could discover the foundation of her life's purpose. This request to run with God, therefore, goes hand in hand with the request for his kiss.

The desire to change the world arises naturally from the blessing given to humankind in the Garden of Eden. After they were blessed as God's beloved children, Adam and Eve were told to be fruitful and multiply. Essentially, they were commissioned to expand the family of the Trinity across the world and cultivate Eden's peace wherever they went.

All gifts and passions spring from this heavenly charge. Unfortunately, our personal gifts can easily become self-serving when used to fill a sense of lack.

That isn't to say we shouldn't use our gifts until we feel complete inner peace. Often, it is by sharing the truth with others that we ourselves grow in it. However, we must move into this calling from the proper foundation. Like the Shulamite, we first take our stand on the rock of Christ's love, fully assured of what was revealed at the cross. This is what the vast majority of the Shulamite's journey has been about. She has been tuning her soul to the original music, thereby aligning her gifts and passions to the right key—all so that she might play his Song with clarity and courage.

As the Song permeates our own souls, the way we utilize our gifts (including the gifts of time and money) will flow from a new conductor. Instead of the old song leader of anxiety or reasoning, a new force will move upon us, leading us into a life of fulfilled destiny.

Our Calling and Destiny

And this destiny and calling is summed up in a phrase many have come to call the "Great Commission."

The Original Commission

Herein lies another term tarnished by guilt-driven religion. Jesus's final words to his followers before his ascension into heaven was to "go and make disciples" (Matthew 28:18-20). Just as he poured his life into them, they were to go and do the same for others. This was the call motivating the Shulamite's prayer when she asked early on for the grace to "run" with God to the nations, bringing them the kiss of his love as well.

This mandate from Jesus—which has been given to his believing "Shulamites" throughout the history of the church—ties back to what was foreshadowed in the Garden, when Adam and Eve were commissioned to multiply. As we've pointed out, the blessing of Genesis 1 was not the commission itself. The blessing is what empowered the commission. We are loved and blessed before we *do* anything for God. This is our foundation as we rise to become runners of grace and truth.

When Jesus gave his commission, the first thing he said to do was to immerse people into "the name of the Father, Son, and Holy Spirit." This is what the religious term *baptize* means. It was never about getting people to join a religious institution. It was about plunging humanity back into their family origin. It is reconnecting people to the very spark of creation. It's the call to true fellowship and healthy family—to the rediscovery of what was lost in Eden.

Jesus's commission is not a military conquest, nor is it some religious labor driven by a harsh taskmaster. Rather, it is a grand adventure with our Best Friend, where we go and awaken other brothers and sisters to the wonders of love, reconciling them with their true name and with the true nature of their Divine

Family. It is where we help people discover the same treasures of revelation for themselves.

This is what the Shulamite taps into as her poetry draws to a close…

> *Let us arise and run to the vineyards of your people*
> *and see if the budding vines of love are now in full bloom.*
> *We will discover if their passion is awakened.*
> *There I will display my love for you.*
> —Song 7:12 TPT

Day Twenty-Eight: Rising from the Wilderness

The eighth chapter of Solomon's Song holds mysteries far beyond the scope of this book. In a frail attempt to nudge you out into its infinite waters, I'll lay out just a few thoughts here. But I pray the sail of your heart is lifted so you can catch the wind that will carry you much farther than my words can.

We'll pick it up in the fifth verse:

> *Who is this coming up from the wilderness*
> *Leaning on her Beloved?...*

The Shulamite is the awakened human soul and the divine counterpart to the Son of God. Here at the end, we find her in full partnership with the Creator, leaning upon him with a deep and proven assurance even as she steps into this great destiny of expanding Eden's borders across the earth.

She comes up from the same wilderness we saw earlier in the vision of a crowned and crucified King. This whole book has been an ascension out of the wilderness of religion and death. Our main character has been learning to wake up to the fact that she is in union with the One who already rose up out of these things.

You may remember from our first visit to the wilderness the mystery hidden in the word *kalah*, found in its alternate meanings—"perfect" and "bride." Interestingly enough, we find a similar thing happening in the wilderness once more—literally, in the word *wilderness* itself.

The Hebrew word for wilderness is *midbār*, usually translated as a deserted place. However, the word can also be rendered as "mouth." Some believe these two meanings are linked because the desert was a place where people heard the voice of God (see Hosea 2:14). Whatever the reason, the double meaning of *midbār* holds a remarkable revelation here at the Song's grand finale.

Hidden Throughout the Music

Think about it. We were launched into this whole venture after the Shulamite requested the kisses of his "mouth." We quickly discovered this awakening kiss is the Word of Christ—it is the reality of his death, resurrection, and ascension—the means by which God redeemed us back to the original word he spoke over humanity:

You are my beloved child in whom I am well-pleased!

It turns out her entire journey has been one long encounter with this kiss. She's been consumed by it, becoming one with the eternal truth pouring from God's lips. Therefore, we can rightfully translate this part of the poem as saying, *"Who is this rising from the mouth of God?"*

Like Jonah getting kissed by a whale, the Shulamite was kissed and swallowed by grace! Then, like the prophet in the belly of the whale for three days, she was given the revelation of being buried in the ground with Christ. In his death, she died. In his resurrection, she lives. Now, no matter what it feels like, no matter how things appear, she knows she is one with the resurrected Son of God.

Finally, like Jonah was spit out of the fish's mouth to go on a mission of mercy to a lost and dark nation, the Shulamite is being released from God's mouth to become his poetry to the world. She goes to the forgotten places to share the brilliant and sparkling message of new life in Jesus. Indeed, she has *become* the message.

Or we might say she has become God's kiss.

The Word of Our Testimony

All this happened after the Shulamite accepted the fact that her false and twisted self was a lie—a lie that was buried in the ground with Jesus. This false self was painted with the imagery of a veiled prostitute—one whose identity is hidden and who engages in an act of paid "love."

We saw how she sought the broad paths of man within the city of religion, and how the kiss of true love was the only way to wake her up from this burdensome spell. This kiss came through her communion with the King, where she learned to adjust her striving, out-of-tune heart to the frequency of grace. As a result, she is now able to sing its message to a world still caught up in the lie. This is what begins to happen as the Song wraps up its final verses:

> *Put me like a seal over your heart,*
> *Like a seal on your arm.*
> *For love is as strong as death,*
> *Jealousy is as severe as Sheol;*
> *Its flashes are flashes of fire,*
> *The very flame of the Lord.*
> –Song 8:6

The Shulamite sings this out as an ambassador for the King. In other words, this verse is actually the song of Jesus as he gives an invitation to the world through the lips of his awakened bride. She carries the victorious revelation of his love and now calls people to let Jesus be a "seal" over their own hearts.

This is the Great Commission in action. These words connect with the call for people to be immersed into the family of God, where they receive what the New Testament calls the "seal" of the Holy Spirit (Ephesians 1:13). The Spirit of God is the kiss of God, and it is only through an encounter with this living kiss that a soul can awaken to its identity and go on to fulfill its destiny.

Such is the treasure we've discovered on this scavenger hunt through God's creation. It is the revelation not only of who we are but of what our divine purpose is. The Spirit of God is then the seal that confirms and ignites all of this into our everyday lives so that we can take it all home with us.

The Shulamite embraced this seal for herself, and now she wants others to know its transforming power. She invites others into this same discovery of the truth. With that, she goes on to describe something of utmost importance she learned along the way:

> *Many waters cannot quench love,*
> *Nor will rivers overflow it;*
> *If a man were to give all the riches of his house for love,*
> *It would be utterly despised.*
> –Song 8:7

God's love is unbreakable and enduring. It will never fade and never give up. Furthermore, his love can never be earned or bought. The unfailing love of the Father is simply who he is. It is the constant truth of his being, revealed most clearly in the suffering death of his Son, Jesus.

Such love can only be received. Baptism, or immersion into water, is simply the way we outwardly show we've received this love as we embrace our death and resurrection with Jesus. When a person truly accepts this grace, the Spirit floods their inner being and causes the original image of God to break loose like fruit in a garden. The Spirit marks their heart like a signet ring pressing upon wax with a seal of authority, confirming who they really are. From there, they are called to be part of a growing family of other awakened sons and daughters with the commission to go out and gather more.

The Shulamite is part of this growing circle of life, and thus she carries the good news to the world—along with the call for true "repentance." But there's another word that's been corrupted by the systems of the world. Originally, this term was about a change of perspective—one that leads us to turn back to the One who has already accepted us. It was a serious and yet joyful invitation into rest.

That brings us to the next few verses of the Song, where we hear about "a little sister" (verse 8). This part refers to those who are not yet as spiritually mature as the Shulamite. Some are like an open "door," ready to receive the message of Jesus, while others are like a closed "wall," resisting his grace (verse 9).

Which leads us to the final words of the Shulamite. In the tenth verse, she gives her testimony in a poetic nutshell. She reminisces about her work in the vineyards of religion and how she found freedom through the love of her Shepherd. She says there was a time when she too was a "wall," unreceptive and closed to the love of God, but—

then I became in his eyes as one who finds peace.

If you remember, the Shulamite's name is the feminine version of the King's name. *Solomon* and *Shulamite* come from the same root word—*shalom*—which means peace, wholeness, and completion. *Shalom* is the essence of Eden, and it is at the center of the blessing bestowed upon humanity. If you've been tracking with us, this is how the King has always seen her and how he's always spoken of her, even when her faith wavered.

Now, as an awakened soul, she recounts how she became *in his eyes* as one who finds *shalom*. By discovering his constant view of her, the Shulamite found the true meaning of her name. In his eyes, she saw her own reflection! She found the "root word" of her existence. The origin of her life is the enduring love of God, and this was established before the beginning of time. Her acceptance of this love is how she finally found the peace her heart always longed for.

Messengers of the Song

A secret garden lies hidden within all humanity. Along with our true name, this garden is locked behind a deceptive veil that can only be torn down by the sword of Christ's mouth. When a soul is immersed into the waters of grace, that sword is released. They arise from the mouth of God and are empowered by the Spirit to help others break free as well.

The Shulamite now dwells in this garden, enjoying the bliss of her union with Christ. Her voice has become a vessel to help other people experience this garden with her, which is why the King says the following words next:

> *O you who sit in the gardens,*
> *My companions are listening for your voice—*
> *Let me hear it!*
> –Song 8:13

The "companions" are those throughout the world who need to hear the life-giving message of grace. They need to hear the message of truth from our own lives. And so, the King longs to hear the Shulamite articulate the message in her own voice and through her own unique story.

This is what he longs for in each of us as well.

May you, dear reader, be swallowed up by this same kiss of truth. May it ignite a garden of awakened fruit throughout the terrain of your soul. And even when there appears to be a wilderness around you, may the truth of God's original blessing speak louder than any other voice:

You are his perfect and beloved child...

...and you make him feel *real good inside*.

Selah

During our first divine pause, you were invited to inhale the breath and kiss of God. Return now to that sacred invitation. Breathe in, and as you do, imagine his love sweeping into the deepest places of your being—filling you, holding you, healing you.

Then, with each exhale, release that love into the world around you. Let your breath carry his presence—first into the room where you sit, then further still, into your neighborhood, your city, the nations.

Ask the Lord to open your heart to the world he so deeply loves. Ask for fresh revelation: *What does it look like to release your kiss, Lord?*

Wait. Listen. Let him show you his heart for others—his compassion, his longing, his delight.

And remember: your calling to impact the world will always flow from this place of being loved. You never move past the need to be kissed by God. You never graduate from grace. The overflow only comes from abiding:

"Just as the Father has loved me, I have also loved you; abide in my love."
–John 15:9–

Stay here a moment longer. Abide in his delightful love for you. Let it wash over your heart and fill you until it overflows. The *overture* is beginning—but it starts with stillness, affection, and rest.

OVERTURE:
SCAVENGER HUNT (BACK) TO JERUSALEM

As I wrote this book, I began to sense a deeper thread woven through my stories from Israel and other parts of Asia—something more than I had first realized. It connects to the great mystery I mentioned earlier: the mystery of the "mother" in the poem.

One hundred years ago, in the early twentieth century, a small group of Asian believers received a vision from Jesus to bring the Gospel back to the place where it all began. This became known as the **Back to Jerusalem** vision. The Chinese church felt commissioned to carry the message of Christ to the nations between China and Israel. This meant going into some of the most dangerous and hardest-to-reach places on the planet.

Amazingly, this vision came more than twenty years before the modern nation of Israel resurrected from the ashes of history. In the wake of global birth pangs and two world wars, Israel reemerged against all odds, with the city of Jerusalem following soon after. Before anyone dreamed this was possible, a small group of believers felt called to a mission that would take several generations to fulfill. They would take the Gospel to all the places that had yet to hear it, believing this work would culminate—unbeknownst to them at the time—in the newly resurrected city of Jerusalem.

Here's where this connects to the Song of all songs. Look again at the final chapter, this time in the second verse:

The Kiss of Christ

*I would lead you and bring you
into the house of my mother,
who used to instruct me...*

In the sixth chapter, the Shulamite awakened to her union with God and began to express this with newfound confidence. In chapter seven, she longs to go to the forgotten places and spiritual vineyards of the world. This was followed in chapter eight by a prayer for boldness—and a request to bring her divine Lover back *"into the house of my mother."*

As we saw earlier, one of the main meanings of the "mother" in the Song of Songs is the nation of Israel. Israel is the one who "used to instruct" us in the way of the law before we encountered the revelation of grace (Galatians 3). It is the place where the Spirit-kiss of God was first poured out—a kiss that has circled the globe ever since. And now, in this final prayer, we see the awakened bride longing to bring Christ back to where it all began.

Just as the growing church in Asia responded to the ancient call, so too are we invited into this divine procession—to carry the Gospel of grace, the proclamation of Christ's finished work, to every nation under heaven. And as the melody of redemption travels the earth, it begins to echo back to its origin.

This is not merely about a return to physical Jerusalem—though that city rests close to the heart of God. It is about the consummation of a greater harmony: the whole earth awakened to the Song of the Ages.

Go Deeper into the Song

The Kiss of Christ is a gentle introduction to the hidden treasures of Solomon's Song. But the journey doesn't end here.

In his three-part series ***The Song of the Ages***, Nick Padovani dives in verse by verse, exploring the mystery of Christ and the awakening of identity woven throughout this ancient poem. Across three volumes, readers are invited into a deeper encounter with the Divine Romance—one that speaks to the heart, renews the mind, and calls forth a life of radiant purpose.

If *The Kiss of Christ* helped you tune in to the divine melody, *The Song of the Ages* will help you live in its rhythm.

Available now on Amazon and other online retailers

Visit **www.EyesOpenPress.com** for even more resources.

We also have an online magazine and media ministry called *Elisha's Riddle*.

Finished work, presence-driven, identity-based resources for God's kids.

Visit
www.ElishasRiddle.com

Nick Padovani is a husband and father of three precious daughters. He serves as the lead pastor of a flourishing spiritual community in northern New Jersey.

In 2005, Nick experienced a life-changing encounter with the grace of God—an awakening that reshaped the course of his life. Since then, he has been devoted to proclaiming the truth of God's unfathomable grace to the nations. His ministry has reached from secular college campuses to non-profits, from local churches to underground gatherings in the 10/40 window.

Nick is also the founder of *Eyes Open Press*, a publishing ministry dedicated to spreading the message of Christ's finished work.

www.ingramcontent.com/pod-product-compliance
Lightning Source LLC
Chambersburg PA
CBHW020530080526
44583CB00013B/810